INTERNET POLICIES AND ISSUES

THE FIRST RESPONDER NETWORK (FIRSTNET)

ELEMENTS, ISSUES, PROGRESS

INTERNET POLICIES AND ISSUES

Additional books in this series can be found on Nova's website under the Series tab.

Additional e-books in this series can be found on Nova's website under the e-book tab.

INTERNET POLICIES AND ISSUES

THE FIRST RESPONDER NETWORK (FIRSTNET)

ELEMENTS, ISSUES, PROGRESS

MARGARET SAUNDERS
EDITOR

nova publishers
New York

Library of Congress Cataloging-in-Publication Data

ISSN: 2158-1517

ISBN: 978-1-63483-850-4

Published by Nova Science Publishers, Inc. † New York

CONTENTS

PREFACE

The First Responder Network Authority (FirstNet) is a federal agency that includes private sector and other non-federal representation on its board of directors. FirstNet was created by Congress with provisions in Title VI (Spectrum Act) of the Middle Class Tax Relief and Job Creation Act of 2012 to ensure the deployment and operation of a nationwide, broadband network for public safety communications. It is established as an "independent authority" within the National Telecommunications and Information Administration (NTIA), part of the Department of Commerce. There are many challenges for public safety leaders and policymakers in establishing the framework for a nationwide network that meets state, local, tribal and territorial needs for robust, interoperable emergency communications. Currently, for example, state emergency communications needs are typically met by separate networks using different technologies. Furthermore, each state has its own laws and procedures for building, managing, and funding communications infrastructure. Among the challenges facing FirstNet is establishing a governance model that accommodates current investments and future needs of its clients without compromising the coherence of a national network. This book discusses the elements, issues, and progress made by FirstNet.

In: The First Responder Network (FirstNet) ISBN: 978-1-63483-850-4
Editor: Margaret Saunders

Chapter 1

THE FIRST RESPONDER NETWORK (FIRSTNET) AND NEXT-GENERATION COMMUNICATIONS FOR PUBLIC SAFETY: ISSUES FOR CONGRESS*

Linda K. Moore

SUMMARY

Congress included provisions in the Middle Class Tax Relief and Job Creation Act of 2012 (P.L. 112-96) for planning, building, and managing a new, nationwide, broadband network for public safety communications, by creating the First Responder Network Authority (FirstNet). The act allocated 10 MHz of additional radio frequency spectrum to accommodate the new network and required that the Federal Communications Commission (FCC) assign a license to FirstNet, comprising the newly designated frequencies and 10 MHz previously assigned to states by the FCC for public safety use. In addition, the act designated federal appropriations of over $7 billion for the network and other public safety needs. These funds are provided through new revenue from the auction of licenses to the commercial sector in other spectrum bands.

---

* This is an edited, reformatted and augmented version of a Congressional Research Service publication R42543, prepared for Members and Committees of Congress, dated May 7, 2015.

The establishment of FirstNet is an important step toward reaching what has been a national goal since September 11, 2001: the provision of interoperable communications for first responders. The immediate goal for FirstNet is to provide a broadband network to carry data, although it will provide an option for voice communications as well. Mission critical voice communications, which require higher levels of quality of service, will, in most states, be available only over Land Mobile Radio (LMR) networks operating on narrowband frequencies that are under the jurisdiction of state and local public safety agencies. States will likely need to continue to invest in and maintain their narrowband networks and may at the same time be obliged to fund some part of the state build-out for FirstNet.

The cost of constructing and maintaining a nationwide network is estimated by many experts to be in the tens of billions of dollars over the long term. The cost of acquiring core network elements needed to provide required functions nationwide is estimated at under $10 million; most of the cost for FirstNet is in deploying and maintaining towers and related infrastructure in states and communities. The law anticipates that some of these costs will be covered by partnerships that permit commercial access to FirstNet's spectrum. How much of the benefit of these partnerships will accrue to FirstNet and how much will be available to the states for state-owned and operated networks in their jurisdictions is unknown. Information available to the public indicates that FirstNet intends to discourage states from building and operating their own networks within FirstNet, in part by limiting the amount of spectrum available for this purpose. FirstNet has taken the position that state autonomy in network design decisions and management will jeopardize FirstNet's ability to provide a network that meets its coverage and service goals. In seeking economies of scale and cost savings for its own business model, however, FirstNet may be transferring costs and risks to states. In the long term, these costs may hinder state and local investment in services generally categorized as the Internet of Things.

The governance model chosen by FirstNet is a federalized, centrally planned and directed network, bolstered by federal procurement practices that limit states to a consultative role. A risk in choosing this model is that states may consider the federal presence excessive and cease to cooperate with FirstNet, jeopardizing the purpose of the network.

INTRODUCTION

The First Responder Network Authority (FirstNet) is a federal agency that includes private sector and other non-federal representation on its board of directors. FirstNet was created by Congress with provisions in Title VI

(Spectrum Act) of the Middle Class Tax Relief and Job Creation Act of 2012 (P.L. 112-96) to ensure the deployment and operation of a nationwide, broadband network for public safety communications. It is established as an "independent authority"[1] within the National Telecommunications and Information Administration (NTIA), part of the Department of Commerce.

In addition to establishing the structure and goals for FirstNet, Congress provided $7 billion for costs related to planning and deploying the broadband network, and a $135 million grant program to assist states with plans to connect to FirstNet's broadband network.[2] These funds are provided from revenue realized through auctioning licenses for radio frequency spectrum, as designated in the act. The anticipated cost of building and operating a nationwide core broadband network— and the interoperable radio networks that connect to it—is significantly in excess of the amount appropriated. The act therefore provides for public-private partnerships with FirstNet or with states, and for fees (charged to states and other users) to ensure that FirstNet becomes self-sustaining. To attract private sector partners, FirstNet can offer access to its assets, including radio frequency spectrum capacity, in return for financial payment or other support. FirstNet holds a license for 20 MHz of broadband spectrum,[3] assigned by the Federal Communications Commission (FCC), as required by the act. The act allows states that meet specified requirements to lease spectrum from FirstNet and thereby negotiate their own partnerships that share spectrum in Radio Area Networks for their state or region. The viability of state-managed partnerships depends in large part on the amount of spectrum that will be made available to the state.

There are many challenges for public safety leaders and policymakers in establishing the framework for a nationwide network that meets state, local, tribal and territorial needs for robust, interoperable emergency communications. Currently, for example, state emergency communications needs are typically met by separate networks using different technologies. Furthermore, each state has its own laws and procedures for building, managing, and funding communications infrastructure. Among the challenges facing FirstNet is establishing a governance model that accommodates current investments and future needs of its clients without compromising the coherence of a national network.

Issues for Congress

FirstNet officials face enormous pressure to produce a functional network in a timely manner, reflecting widespread concerns that public safety communications will not be adequate for response and recovery if a catastrophic national emergency occurs. Building momentum after a slow start in setting up the organization, it is possible that FirstNet, working closely with the NTIA, is now opting for expediency at the expense of states' own public safety goals. For example, much of the available information about the role of states in managing networks in their jurisdiction is—at this point in time—vague, with a heavy emphasis on proposals, drafts, and works-in-progress.

FirstNet may not have fully evaluated the consequences of a centralized, closely controlled network over the long term. In particular, states that may be considering building their own networks, within FirstNet, may find that the final plans proposed to them, after the contracts are awarded in late 2016 or 2071, are too federal-centric. State governors may at this point turn to their Members of Congress for assistance in gaining more control over the operations within their own jurisdictions. At this point, however, revising the contracts negotiated by the FirstNet Board of Directors may be difficult and costly.

Both the Government Accountability Office and the Inspector General of the Department of Commerce have found fault with the decision-making process at FirstNet and the level of oversight by the NTIA.[4] If these faults appear to be a trend, Congress may consider the value of greater vigilance over the planning process for the deployment of the Nationwide Public Safety Broadband Network that it created. For example, a number of economic decisions that claim to justify federal control are not supported by public circulation of the economic modeling.

FirstNet Network Strategy

Achievements since the FirstNet board first met officially in September 2012 include a number of Requests for Information (RFI), notably the September 2014 *Request for Information for Comprehensive Network Solution(s).*[5] This document proposes a comprehensive broadband network solution for FirstNet that would reach from core network management requirements to include local area networks in many communities, as well as some devices used to access the network.[6] A *Second Notice,* issued by the Department of Commerce for comment on March 9, 2015,[7] provides FirstNet's perspective on the intent of Congress in enacting language that allows states to build their own network. The discussion in the *Second Notice* also supplements the *Public Notice on Statutory Interpretations*,[8] issued in September 2014. A number of important issues are raised in these formal statements of proposed interpretation, including possible definitions of "public safety" and "rural" to be used in negotiations with potential commercial partners.

A third public notice[9] concerning the definition of "public safety" was released after a FirstNet board meeting on April 24, 2015.[10] Also on April 24, the proposed acquisition approach[11] and the draft Request for Proposal(s) (RFP)[12] were considered in a closed meeting. The draft RFP builds on proposals from previous notices and RFIs. The planning process for 2015-2016 is centered on circulating the draft Request for Proposal(s) and a final RFP. FirstNet has announced that the contract or contracts will be awarded through the Federal Acquisition Regulation (FAR) process[13] sometime in late 2016 or in 2017. FirstNet has indicated that it may negotiate federal procurement contracts for services at the state or regional level as well as nationwide.[14]

As currently envisioned, after the initial contracts are awarded, the winning bidders will provide individual proposals for each state for the deployment and operation of FirstNet's broadband service within that state. Negotiations between each state and FirstNet may lead to contract modifications. Some observers have estimated that the process, to be properly executed with all states and territories, may take as much as three years. The finalized contract terms for each state are then likely to be submitted for final review by the state. Submission of the final proposals to state governments is expected to trigger the required 90-day decision period for each governor to accept FirstNet's proposal or to opt out in expectation of separately building a Radio Area Network. The act's opt-out requirements as described in the Spectrum Act are discussed in a later section, "State Participation: The Opt-Out Provision."

According to FirstNet, "key goals are to meet the needs of public safety and to provide extensive coverage so Federal subscribers and other public safety users can count on the network when they are on the job."[15] Network coverage includes deployable units, such as vehicles equipped to connect with the network, and local area networks operated by FirstNet. "Incident commanders and officials will have local control over the network so, for example, they can assign users and talk groups and determine who can access applications."[16] The underlying premise of the strategy is that the chosen network solutions will allow FirstNet to "control and operate" national and regional core network infrastructure, Radio Area Networks (RANs) in states that opt-in, as well as devices, applications, and other functions.[17] To achieve this level of coverage, FirstNet's "acquisition strategy centers on maximizing the network's value to public safety while meeting its financial sustainability obligations under the Act."[18] The intent of this network design is to maximize the value of spectrum for the benefit of the greater good by capturing the full value of the spectrum, nationwide, in order to provide sufficient funding for rural coverage.[19]

Draft Request for Proposals

The documents supplied for the draft RFP provide detailed information for potential contract bidders. Each document covers a portion of the many guidelines and requirements for comprehensive network solutions. These are described as including

> deployment and provisioning of a nationwide core; all radio access components (RAN) for opt-in states; backhaul, aggregation and national transport networks and data centers; a device ecosystem; network infrastructure; deployable capabilities; operational and business support systems; an application ecosystem and network services; as well as integration, maintenance, and operational services required to function fully as an operational wireless Third Generation Partnership Program (3GPP) Long Term Evolution (LTE) NPSBN. FirstNet's objective is to maximize the network's value to public safety while meeting its financial sustainability obligations under the Act.[20]

To increase competition among potential bidders, FirstNet proposes in the *Special Notice* to allow bidders for federal contracts to be either for a nationwide network, covering all the requirements—and others described in the draft documents—for a comprehensive network solution, or for regional networks that may cover one or more states or regions, including territories.[21] One of the appendices, C-2, which covers service level agreements for radio access network integration for opt-out states, was not posted on April 27 with the other documents. According to an amendment to the *Special Notice*, it requires more input from states and vendors and "may be provided at a later date or in a subsequent RFP."

The acquisition documents consider key factors such as the value provided for excess network capacity, speed to market, public safety program objectives, and rural coverage.[22] The draft *Special Notice* is complex, highly technical, and is asking for comments as well as indications of interest from potential contractors or subcontractors. Comments are due by July 27, 2015, and may be reflected in the final Request for Proposal when it is issued to potential bidders.

State Radio Area Networks

Since September 11, 2001, state and local agencies—aided by federal grant programs—have invested in improving the reliability and interoperability of mission critical voice communications over Land Mobile Radio (LMR) networks. The 2014 National Emergency Communications Plan prepared by the Department of Homeland Security emphasizes the need to continue investment in these networks to provide communication for first responders until such time as FirstNet is deployed and capable of handling mission-critical voice communications over broadband.[23] These networks may also be essential for local and state backup service when access to FirstNet has been preempted by a large-scale emergency, or they may be an alternative to using FirstNet.[24]

Although many details have not been made public, the general architecture of FirstNet's broadband network has been presented at numerous public events and is available on the FirstNet website.[25] The network design shows what is referred to as a heterogeneous network, or HetNet. It depicts the Radio Access Network to include both macro and micro networks. In simple terms, high towers with base stations, known as eNodeB in LTE network design, are referred to by the wireless industry as a macro network; a variety of small cell[26] network designs are referred to as micro networks. The macro network is often described as providing coverage over distance and the micro network as providing capacity as well as extra coverage at the local level.[27]

Micro Networks

The trend in the evolution of micro networks is depicted in *Figure 1*. In this configuration, the micro network has become the predominate provider of mobile communications coverage and capacity through contiguous small cell networks. The tower of the macro network (eNodeB) assures connectivity and provides additional coverage. Small cell networks are by and large autonomous, providing coverage for their area and connecting to other small cell networks or cellular towers when needed. These micro networks are local in nature but fully interoperable across wide geographic areas. For FirstNet, a network strategy that shifts the majority of routine, public safety mobile communications onto shared spectrum in small cell networks will free much of the 20 MHz spectrum license for secondary use. Only in times of a major emergency would public safety users make heavy demands on the macro network and spectrum licensed to FirstNet.

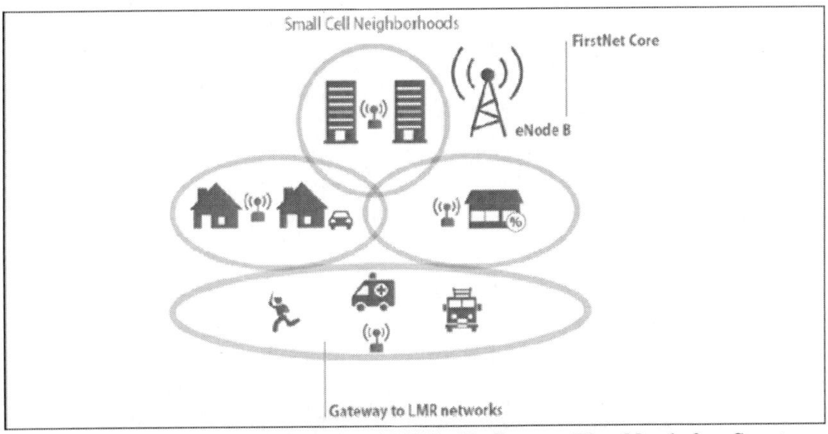

Source: 4G Americas, Meeting the 1000X Challenge: The Need for Spectrum, Technology and Policy Innovation, October 2013, Figure AI-1, p. 130, http://www.4gamericas.org/documents/2013_4G%20Americas%20Meeting%20the%201000x%20Challenge%2010%204%2013_FINAL.pdf.
Revised by CRS to include a small cell deployment for public safety operations.

Figure 1. Small Cell Neighborhood Micro Network.

In an LTE network, it is the eNodeB macro coverage infrastructure—not the micro network—that requires a significant spectrum assignment to operate efficiently. During the period 2011-2012, when the Spectrum Act was drafted and enacted, the Radio Area Network would have consisted primarily of high-site towers with base stations (eNodeB).[28] Since the Spectrum Act was passed, communications technologies have evolved in ways not fully anticipated at the time.[29] Congress, therefore, may have assumed that a state with a successful plan to opt out and create its own public-private partnership would be granted a statewide license for 20 MHz to operate a Radio Area Network using eNodeB towers and base stations. Micro networks, however, can operate within the 20 MHz assignment, essentially sharing the spectrum, but may require no more than 1.5 x 1.5 MHz for a basic LTE network. Therefore, if FirstNet decides that only micro network capacity will be made available for a state-operated Radio Area Network, then the state will have a sub-license for a relatively small amount of spectrum that may be difficult—perhaps impossible—to leverage in a public-private partnership.

State and Community Network Participation

The following discussion focuses on key statements from FirstNet that seem to indicate the agency's current plans for state, tribal, territorial, and local participation in the network. FirstNet may later choose to alter its plans.[30]

FirstNet's deployment strategy reportedly will:

- Include state-based eNodeB's in FirstNet's core services, thereby bringing the entire 20 MHz spectrum license under the full control of FirstNet and its federal contractors.[31] This decision, if implemented, represents a change in an earlier statement that proposes including the eNode B as part of the Radio Area Network.[32]
- Provide local area network capacity and connections as an extension of FirstNet, limiting state authority to providing fill-in capacity for some under-served areas.[33]
- Assign to FirstNet contractors the responsibility of identifying additional partners or subcontractors to act under the authority of the contractor; this might include, for example, negotiating an agreement with a local power company for access to its infrastructure.[34]
- Assign negotiations for access to existing state, local, or tribal infrastructure to contractors, to be pursued after the contract has been issued.[35]

- Extend coverage to rural areas where there is currently little or no commercial service through new, federally funded build-out to the commercial networks of partners chosen through the RFP process.[36]

A major goal of this network design is to maximize the value of spectrum by capturing its full value, nationwide, in order to provide sufficient funding for rural coverage. FirstNet therefore believes that allowing states to build their own RANs "potentially takes with it subscriber fees and/or excess network capacity fees that would have helped fund the FirstNet network in all other states."[37]

Apparently not included in FirstNet's planning process is an analysis of the costs to be assumed by states as a consequence of its business plan. These costs include the continued operation and possible expansion of state and local LMR voice networks; the cost of integration of LMR and broadband infrastructure; the costs of forfeiting to FirstNet the potential economies of scale in network construction and operation; and the cost of lost opportunities for competitions and innovation in wireless services at the state and local level.

RISKS AND REWARDS

FirstNet appears to be making decisions about the network design that are evolving as new information is gathered and analyzed. It claims that a federalized network is the "only solution"[38] that meets its goals of providing nationwide coverage, interoperability, and assured access. In the *Second Notice* it concludes that allowing populous states to opt out of FirstNet and build their own public safety broadband networks, monetizing the value of the 20 MHz of spectrum assigned for that purpose, will beggar their more rural neighbors who cannot so readily capture the value of excess capacity. This is a presumption of market failure that is not supported by information made public by FirstNet and is inconsistent with the many positive analyses of the economic value of small cell networks, community broadband, and the Internet of Things.[39]

The value of economies of scale in building and operating wireless networks has long been recognized by telecommunications experts and policymakers. The FCC, for example, has modified its policies to make it easier for wireless companies to expand through mergers and acquisitions in order to benefit from scale economies.[40] These and related FCC decisions are based on, among other considerations, improving coverage through macro networks to customers for wireless services. When FirstNet refers to the importance of economies of scale, it is apparently referring to geographic coverage through macro networks.[41]

The economics for small cell networks, however, enable profitability by providing economies of scope, with many different types of services to multiple customer segments in a small area.

Economies are provided not through macro network coverage but by micro network capacity to accommodate many customers with different technology needs. Many wireless network experts believe that dense deployments of small cells in an area served by a single eNodeB tower will increase efficiency and reduce costs while increasing capacity to handle many different markets.[42]

Although urbanized areas are seen by many as the primary market for expanding small cell services, the benefits may also be important in rural or remote areas. Experts suggest that, in addition to serving public safety, a rural small cell configuration could support, for example, transportation improvements, education, job search, agricultural and forestry management, new efficiencies in municipal government and services, and economic growth.[43] Economies of scale at the macro level may also be available in states with a low population density. A cost-effective network solution may be achieved by adjacent states combining their resources to provide coverage with eNodeBs and maximizing the utility of small cell networks at the local level. For state and local public safety agencies, maximizing the value of spectrum may be less important than achieving sufficient levels of scale and scope to meet their requirements.

FirstNet refers to the need to monetize the value of its spectrum holdings to expand coverage, based on the existing commercial footprint for LTE, not the footprint of statewide or local public safety networks. It does not estimate the value to states and communities of small cell networks and the wireless component of community broadband that may be transferred to FirstNet's commercial partners. FirstNet's plans appear to capture for its own use most of the value of spectrum used to provide both coverage and capacity. This value is unknown but potentially far greater than what FirstNet can lawfully[44] spend on improving its network or by reducing user fees. The excess value of the spectrum and access to local markets that FirstNet is using to barter for goods and services, therefore, will in most cases go to FirstNet's contractual partners, not to the states and communities intended by the act to be the primary beneficiaries of FirstNet's actions.

FirstNet appears to have documented the benefits but not the risks associated with their decisions. Some of the more salient pros and cons of FirstNet's strategy are summarized below.

Advantages of FirstNet's Comprehensive Network Strategy

Advantages of a federalized network, cited by FirstNet,[45] include:

- Swift execution. Adding public safety access to existing commercial LTE infrastructure provides a turn-key solution for immediate access to a potentially large number of public safety agencies, federal agencies, and others;
- Extension of LTE service to rural areas that currently have no commercial broadband service and might not have public safety communications coverage;
- Streamlined access for federal partners. Instead of negotiating with each state or regional network, federal agencies need only negotiate with FirstNet to gain immediate access to the entire network;
- National reach in times of emergency and assured access to federal incident commanders and officials;
- Economies of Scale. FirstNet requires full control of many assets in order to maximize their value throughout the network; and
- Sustainability. Development of small cell networks under FirstNet's control allows for most traffic to be off-loaded on to local networks that require minimal spectrum, freeing spectrum for customers with a higher dollar-value for FirstNet.

Other Advantages

A number of advantages offered by FirstNet could be available in many other governance or business models. These include:

- Operation of core network (Evolved Packet Core) services such as enforcement of rules for interoperability and other policies and rules, operations, performance and security management, and subscriber databases;

- Purchasing power. Negotiated discounts for equipment through buying cooperatives;
- Research and development, standardization, and negotiations with standards bodies;
- Widespread adoption of broadband technologies to improve, enhance, and extend the effectiveness of emergency responders; and
- Development of best practices for cybersecurity and enforcement of network security procedures.

Disadvantages of FirstNet's Comprehensive Network Strategy

Some disadvantages of a federalized network might be:

- Loss of state autonomy. States have a consultative role but many decisions rest with FirstNet. States also lose control of spectrum assets, potentially limiting their ability to develop capabilities and services that are of value to them but not to FirstNet's customers for nationwide service;
- Devaluation of state and federally funded investments in existing public safety communications networks. Although contractors may, after receiving a contract, negotiate with states and localities for access to their assets, the value and availability of those assets have not been openly stated in the FirstNet planning process;
- Displacement of local competitors by the FirstNet contractor in local and state broadband development. Smaller communities may not be able to generate sufficient business for two or more broadband service providers. To achieve financially viable programs, they might be restricted to using the incumbent (FirstNet) provider;
- Displacement of partners for broadband development. Desirable partners (such as a rural utility) may not be available for local projects because of contractual obligations to FirstNet;
- Loss of market power for state public safety customers. If fees from state and local public safety agencies are a small part of FirstNet's revenue stream, states lose some of their bargaining power in negotiating for improved services or other requests; and
- Increased risk through lack of diversified assets. Risks include operational risks such as a system wide failure or cyberattack;

financial risks such as monopoly pricing; competitive risks in some markets controlled by FirstNet contractors that may lead to reduced innovation; and the risk of poor management decisions with systemwide impact.

State reactions in weighing risks and rewards of network participation may lead to another risk: limited participation, negating much of the intended value of FirstNet.

STATE PARTICIPATION: THE OPT-OUT PROVISION

Every state has one or more agencies that plan for public safety, homeland security, and emergency communications. To be eligible for grants from the Department of Homeland Security, states have established a Statewide Interoperability Coordinator (SWIC) to administer its Statewide Communication Interoperability Plan (SCIP).[46] SCIPs are written to conform with federal guidelines and requirements, such as the National Emergency Communications Plan. FirstNet is required to consult with regional, state, tribal, and local authorities regarding decisions such as those concerning the costs of the policies it formulates, as required in the law, including expenditures for the core network, placement of towers, coverage areas, security, and priority access for local users. Consultation will be through a state-selected coordinator as specified in the act.[47] Appointment of an individual or governmental body as the Single Point of Contact (SPOC) is required as a condition of state participation and eligibility to receive grants established by the act.[48]

States may decide to use the existing SWIC as the required single point-of-contact or may choose to appoint a separate coordinator. Each state and other participants have appointed a coordinator to work directly with FirstNet.[49] The coordinator (SPOC) is responsible for managing FirstNet activities in his or her state. Often this includes revising the existing SCIP to include broadband communications.

The governor of each state is to be notified by FirstNet when it has completed its requests for proposals regarding construction, operation, maintenance, and improvement of a nationwide network. The governor or his designee will receive the details of the proposed plans and notification of the amount of funding available to the state if it participates in the FirstNet program.[50]

The act only identifies two options for a state: join FirstNet or build a statewide Radio Access Network subject to the provisions of the act. The act does not include specific provisions for a state that chooses to build its own Radio Access Network without opting out of FirstNet, although providing such an option may be within FirstNet's charter. A state might, for example, choose to build its own data management center or mobile access routers while also sharing FirstNet's infrastructure for regional and national coverage. The act also is silent on whether states may choose to opt out of the broadband network entirely, choosing neither to join FirstNet nor to build a broadband network on the frequencies assigned to FirstNet.[51] Some states may prefer to concentrate their resources on improving mission-critical voice networks and acquire broadband access from a commercial provider or through other means. FirstNet, through its partners, intends to provide service in all states, even if a state chooses not to be a customer or otherwise participate in the network.[52]

The Spectrum Act specifies that a state that chooses to build its own Radio Access Network must submit an alternative plan for construction, operation, maintenance, and improvement of the Radio Access Network within the state. The state must demonstrate to the FCC, which the law requires to review the plan, that its planned Radio Access Network would comply with minimum technical requirements and be interoperable with FirstNet. The state has 90 days to agree to participate or to notify FirstNet, the NTIA, and the FCC of its intent to deploy its own part of the Radio Access Network, and an additional 180 days to provide its plan to the FCC.[53]

If a state's plan is approved it will be eligible to apply for a grant, administered by the NTIA, that will be funded from the Network Construction Fund created by the act. The amount available may be less than what would have been provided if the state had opted in to the FirstNet program, because the grant will be applied only toward building the Radio Access Network and may be subject to matching grant requirements. Approval of the grant is contingent on meeting additional requirements established by the NTIA, including sustainability, timeliness, cost-effectiveness, security, coverage, and services that are comparable to FirstNet.[54] The state would be required to pay a user fee for access to FirstNet's core network.[55] It would not be permitted to enter commercial markets or lease access to its network except through a public-private partnership. Any revenue to the state from a partnership must be used only for costs associated with its broadband network.[56] If a state's plan meets FCC and NTIA requirements, then the NTIA may grant a license to a state to operate on some portion of the FirstNet spectrum.

NTIA GRANT PROGRAMS

The NTIA, in consultation with FirstNet, has responsibility for carrying out two grant programs: the State and Local Implementation Grant Program (SLIGP); and grants from the Network Construction Fund to states that are permitted to build their own Radio Area Networks.

State and Local Implementation Grant Program

The State and Local Implementation Fund was allocated $135 million[57] from the Public Safety Trust Fund for grants to be made available to all 56 states and territories to develop a plan on how to use a nationwide public safety broadband network to meet their emergency communications needs. The distribution of available funds among the states is established by the NTIA, which administers the State and Local Implementation Grant Program in consultation with FirstNet. The program is as a matching grant program. Federal grants from the fund are not to exceed 80% of the projected cost to the state; however, the NTIA may make the decision to waive the matching funds requirement.

The NTIA decided to plan for funding in two phases. Grants for both phases totaled over $116 million. Grants for the initial phase were awarded to 54 of the 56 eligible states and territories in FY2013. The state of Mississippi and the territory of the Northern Mariana Islands did not receive grants. The first phase of funding, totaling about $58 million, has helped states conduct outreach with public safety and state and local officials to determine their needs, gaps, and priorities for public safety wireless broadband and to prepare for formal consultations with FirstNet. Grants in the second phase may be used by states to collect data identifying and prioritizing where public safety broadband coverage is needed; identifying potential users and their capacity needs; detailing current providers and procurement mechanisms; and similar needs.[58] Reportedly,

> NTIA has recently decided no federal grant monies (SLIGP) can be used to explore any option other than "opt in". FirstNet itself recently asked for review of its interpretations of the Law ("second notice"), and those interpretations also tend to restrict the ability of states to explore options to build their own. It is clear NTIA does not want states doing

coverage and financial modeling, even though such work would result in improved FirstNet plans for each state.[59]

Network Construction Fund

The Spectrum Act requires that $7 billion, reduced by the amount needed to establish FirstNet, be available for a Network Construction Fund established in the Treasury to be used by FirstNet for costs associated with building the nationwide network and for grants to states that qualify to build their own networks.[60]

The act effectively creates three types of expenditures from the Network Construction Fund but does not specify how funds would be allocated for (1) expenditures by FirstNet on construction, maintenance, and related expenses to build the nationwide network required in the act; (2) by the NTIA to make payments to states that are participating in FirstNet; and (3) by the NTIA for grants to those states that qualify to build their own Radio Access Networks.[61]

In FirstNet's *Special Notice*, the "Proposed Pricing Methodology" suggests that little or no provision is being made for grants to opt-out states. The notice proposes,

> Potential offerors may be required to propose how much of the $6.5 billion in Government funding that FirstNet will make available is needed to deploy, operate and maintain the NPSBN, based on their proposed solution given the level of value available as described in (2) below. Potential offerors would be required to propose the timing of when the funding is required to achieve the initial operating capability milestones that are detailed in the draft RFP documents.[62]

FirstNet Administrative Expenditures

The FY2014 *Annual Report to Congress*[63] from FirstNet shows operating expenses for the year of $24.4 million, of which $6.2 million was attributed to administrative expenses. The report notes that the Spectrum Act caps administrative expenditures at $100 million for the first 10 years of operation and states the "cap has been identified as a future barrier for FirstNet progress because it is projected to limit administrative costs to impractical levels. Management estimates that to operate within this limitation, FirstNet and the public will have to accept risks to FirstNet operations...." The funding guidance for FY2015 allows for a budget of as much as $120 million, of which up to $21.4 million is anticipated for expenditures on organizational infrastructure, project support, and administrative functions. An additional $22.3 million is projected for planning, consultation, and outreach activities.[64]

The FY2016 budget proposal limit for all expenses is $160 million, which includes funding for approximately 150 Full Time Equivalent employees as well as additional contracting and administrative support.[65]

FirstNet has not made public its projections for annual salaries and expenditures that might be attributed to operating costs or to administrative expenses. A possible yardstick might be the annual expenditures of the NTIA to manage what are referred to as "reimbursable obligations." These funds are provided through fees that the NTIA is authorized to collect for services, such as payments from other federal agencies for spectrum management. These fees support a workforce roughly equivalent in size and purpose (managing technical programs and meeting client needs) to FirstNet. With a work force of 155 Full Time Equivalent employees, annual expenditures attributed to reimbursable operations at the NTIA are estimated at $40.6 million in FY2015 and $42.6 million in FY2016.[66]

An alternative to increasing the amount available for FirstNet administrative expenses would be to give more responsibility to states, tribal authorities, and territories in administering the networks in their states.

GAO STUDY

The Spectrum Act requires that, before the end of FY2022, the Government Accountability Office (GAO) is to recommend to Congress what actions should be taken in regard to the ending of FirstNet's authority, mandated to occur in 2027. Addiitonally, at the request of the Senate Committee on Commerce, Science, and Transportation, GAO has prepared an evaluation of FirstNet's organization, including business decisions contained in the request for proposal; use of commercial, federal, state, local, and tribal infrastructure in deploying the network nationwide; and financial sustainability. GAO presented preliminary findings as testimony at a Commerce Committee hearing on March 11, 2015,[67] and issued a final report on some of these issues on April 28, 2015.[68]

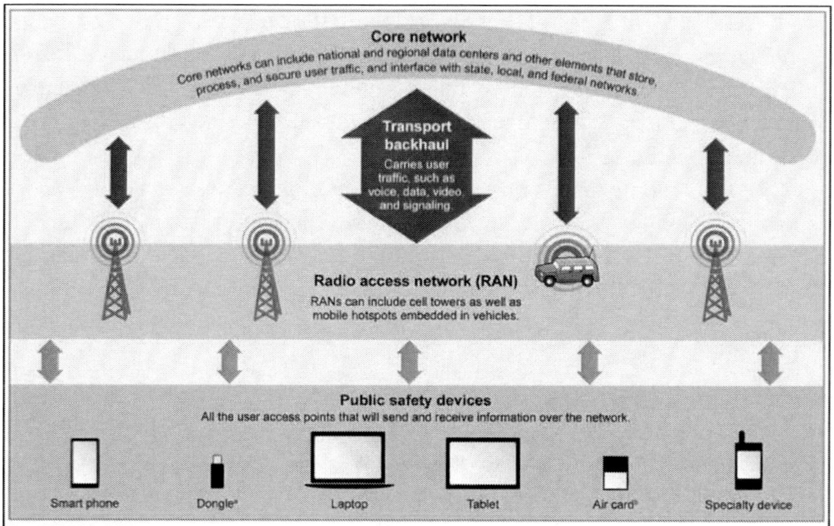

Source: GAO | GAO-15-380T

[a]Generally, "dongles" are small devices that plug into computers and serve as an adapter or as a security measure to enable the use of certain software.

[b]Generally, "air cards" are wireless adapters for sending and receiving data in a cellular network.

Source: GAO, Public Safety Communications: Preliminary Information on FirstNet's Efforts to Establish a Nationwide Broadband Network, GAO-15-380T.

Figure 2. Key Elements of First Responder Network Authority's Public Safety Network, GAO.

The preliminary report included estimates of the cost of building a public safety broadband network from various sources, but no information from FirstNet. The costs were not broken down by key elements, as identified in the report as core network; transport backhaul; Radio Access Network (RAN); and public safety devices. A depiction of the elements, provided in the report, appears in *Figure 2*. This depiction reflects the language in the Spectrum Act, not FirstNet LTE network design proposals. Therefore, Figure 2 does not include small cell networks, unlike the schematics provided by FirstNet in its recent presentations.

In testimony, GAO summarized the progress FirstNet has made in meeting its responsibilities but noted that it had not put in place a number of measures that GAO considers important. Notably, GAO found that FirstNet has not fully assessed the risks associated with its planning efforts (such as conflict of interest); has not established Standards of Conduct; and is not fully evaluating the information from five "early builder" projects.[69]

GAO noted that, as of February 15, 2015, there are over 120 people employed by FirstNet, with a number of positions unfilled. The annual cost of salaries and expenditures that will be required to maintain FirstNet and its outreach programs to states and other customers was not discussed in the preliminary report.

The full report expands on the information provided in testimony. The full report includes, for example, a timeline and other information regarding the development of FirstNet; more details about the "early builder" program; and some insight into FirstNet's planning process. Regarding the interaction of planning and the cost of building the network, GAO's comments include these observations:

- "As part of its planning and market research, FirstNet has developed a cost estimate for its public safety network that met most of the best practices against which we evaluated it."
- "FirstNet's cost estimate, including the assumptions it is based on, are not public because of the highly sensitive nature of the information it contains."
- "We did not assess FirstNet's cost estimate against all the characteristics established in our Cost Estimating and Assessment Guide. Specifically, we did not assess whether FirstNet's estimate was 'credible' or 'accurate' because the estimate and its associated documentation were deemed business sensitive."
- "We did not analyze the quantitative input and output of the cost model because the data included procurement sensitive information, and we would therefore be unable to report our findings in a public report."
- "Therefore we cannot say if the estimate is in line with the credible and accurate characteristics of our Cost Estimating and Assessment Guide."[70]

OIG REPORT ON FIRSTNET

Criticism by a member of the board of FirstNet, in April 2013—regarding a lack of transparency in information provided to the board, and other issues—led to a review of practices by the Office of Inspector General (OIG.).[71] The primary focus of the review had two main objectives, to determine whether the Department of Commerce (DOC)

- had adequate processes in place to ensure that FirstNet Board members properly filed financial disclosures and identified potential conflicts of interest; and
- used appropriate contracting processes and requirements.

The overall finding is that some monitoring procedures were inadequate, including, for example, a finding that "FirstNet contracting practices lacked transparent award competition, sufficient oversight of hiring, adequate monitoring, and procedures to prevent erroneous costs...."[72]

In its review, the OIG looked at the roles of the NTIA, the DOC Office of General Counsel, and two agencies within DOC that were assigned direct responsibilities to assist FirstNet; the Bureau of Census and NIST were asked to award and manage contracts with outside entities to provide assistance to FirstNet. The OIG did not specifically review activities of the NTIA Office of Public Safety Communications, created to assist FirstNet with administrative tasks, including staffing.

The OIG review determined that nearly $11 million had been inappropriately spent, much of it going for consulting work that did not meet contractual definitions of deliverables. The OIG referred to this consulting work as "work products" and questioned the expenditures. The DOC responded that it conducted relevant contracting activities in accordance with federal procurement laws and regulations and monitored performance, and that the contracts produced "first-rate feasibility research, technical analysis, strategic planning, and outreach services from highly specialized consultants, whose work product has laid the groundwork for executing FirstNet's mission."[73]

The OIG made recommendations to the Secretary, the General Counsel, the Chair of FirstNet, and the DOC's Senior Procurement Official regarding various procedures and responsibilities. A joint response from FirstNet, the NTIA, and the General Counsel concurred with the specific recommendations from the OIG, although not all the findings. In general, they defended their actions in the context of unique requirements and time constraints in setting up FirstNet.

The OIG review covered a limited range of issues linked to oversight procedures. Although it did not go into detail, the OIG noted "inconsistent administration"[74] and several instances of significant time lags in the performance of DOC officials. For example, "6 months after the Board began regular meetings, senior NTIA and Office of General Consel officials were still debating [the monitoring] of potential conflicts of interest."[75] OIG found that most of the lapses occurred in the year after the FirstNet board held its first official meeting in September 2012. The review observed that "neither a business plan nor a network plan were completed or delivered to FirstNet during the 1-year performance period of the contracts...."[76]

The OIG has established a team to audit and evaluate FirstNet activities. Additionally, it operates a fraud, waste, and abuse hotline for the Department of Commerce, which has received complaints regarding FirstNet. The OIG conducts follow-up on these complaints.[77]

HIGHLIGHTS OF PROGRESS THROUGH 2014

The complexities of setting up FirstNet as a federal agency are generally accepted as a primary cause of slow progress in its initial months of operation.[78] The pace of activity increased in 2014 and FirstNet was able to show measurable accomplishments by yearend. The planning vehicle that has been shared with the public is an executive summary of a "Roadmap,"[79] adopted by the FirstNet board in March 2014.[80] The Roadmap focuses on milestones needed to develop a definitive business plan and complete state-based plans. The milestones are

- Staff and resource the organization;
- Complete an open, transparent, and complete process for comprehensive network proposals based upon FirstNet LTE performance requirements, operating standards, and certified devices;
- Complete an open, transparent, and competitive process for network equipment and services proposals based on detailed technical requirements, resulting in multiple awards that could supplement or substitute for all or part of a comprehensive network proposal;
- In conjunction with each of the comprehensive network and network equipment and services processes, obtain proposals for covered leasing agreements that will provide value for excess network capacity;
- Complete testing and validation of critical features and functionality of the network;

- Conduct state outreach and complete consultations;[81] and
- Review aggregated information to determine pricing for approval by the NTIA.

At the June 2014 meeting[82] of the FirstNet board the following actions in support of the Roadmap were announced:

- The charter for the Public Safety Advisory Committee (PSAC) was formally adopted. By-laws for the PSAC, required by the act, were adopted at the organizing meeting of the FirstNet Board of Directors on September 25, 2012.[83] There are no requirements in the statute as to the composition of the committee.
- The process for compliance with the National Environmental Policy Act was approved.

In September 2014, the board approved resolutions "designed to generate valuable perspectives from public safety, industry, and the general public on important foundational issues regarding the development of the network." At the same meeting, the board approved a FY2015 budget for FirstNet, not to exceed $120 million. At a subsequent meeting,[84] the Finance Committee approved obligations of $86.2 million, including up to $42.5 million for a comprehensive Request for Proposal (RFP) and some network development activities; $22.3 million on consultation, planning, and outreach activities; and up to $21.4 million on FirstNet organizational infrastructure, project support, and administrative functions. Development of the RFP and consultation programs with states were identified as the "main thrusts" of activities for FY2015.

The Roadmap established four milestones to reach within a year. Actions taken are in brackets.

- Initiate public notice and comment on certain program procedures, policies, and statutory interpretations. [*Public Notice on Statutory Interpretations*, issued September 2014.]
- Release draft request for comprehensive network proposals for offeror comments. [*Comprehensive Network Request for Information and Statement of Objectives*,[85] issued September 2014.]
- Release draft requests for certain network equipment and services proposals for offeror comments.

- Begin formal state consultations. [The first consultation was held with the State of Maryland, July 2014.[86]]

The FirstNet planning process is still evolving and subject to change as the procurement process moves forward. An update of the Roadmap and other activities, including a tentative timeline for 2015, was provided on September 17, 2014, in presentations by FirstNet officials.[87] The published timeline for 2015 shows two parallel tracks that are expected to converge by yearend. Track One shows the ongoing state consultation process. The second, separate, track shows the iterative progress from the RFI to a final Request for Proposal and the awarding of a contract or contracts for the deployment of FirstNet. An important goal for 2015 is to complete the first round of consultations between FirstNet and each state, as well as consultations with tribal authorities, territories, and the District of Columbia. State consultations will continue through 2015, concurrent with the final stages of contract discussions with potential partners.

As FirstNet moves from Requests for Information, to Requests for Proposals, to the awarding of a contract or contracts to deploy and operate its broadband network, it may become clear how the needed technical support and funding for state participation will be supplied.

Discussion of Other Provisions in the Spectrum Act to Improve Public Safety Communications

Following is a discussion of major provisions in the act that pertain to public safety communications, including provisions to improve the nation's 911 emergency call system.[88]

Among federal agencies designated by the act to provide consultation and support are the Federal Communications Commission (FCC), the National Telecommunications and Information Administration (NTIA), the National Institute of Standards and Technology (NIST), and the Office of Emergency Communications (OEC). The FCC manages commercial and non-federal spectrum use, including spectrum allocated to public safety. The NTIA manages federal spectrum resources and, along with NIST, is an agency within the Department of Commerce. OEC is part of the Office of Cybersecurity and Communications, Department of Homeland Security.

Spectrum Assignment

Radio frequency spectrum is an essential resource for wireless communications. The energy in electronic telecommunications transmissions converts airwaves into signals to deliver voice, text, and images. These signal frequencies are allocated for specific purposes, such as television broadcasting or WiFi,[89] and assigned to specific users through licenses. Allocating sufficient spectrum for wireless emergency communications has long been a concern for Congress. The Balanced Budget Act of 1997 (P.L. 105-33), for example, directed the FCC to allocate 24 MHz[90] of spectrum in the 700 MHz band for public safety use.[91]

With the passage of the Spectrum Act, some existing public safety licenses in the 700 MHz band[92] and an additional license for commercial use (known as the D Block)[93]—together totaling 22 MHz—have been re-designated by Congress for a federal license for paired spectrum at 758- 768 MHz and 788-798 MHz, plus guard bands at 768-769 MHz and 798-799 MHz to mitigate interference from adjacent channels. As required by the act, the initial, 10-year license to use these frequencies was assigned by the FCC to FirstNet. It is renewable for an additional 10 years, on condition that FirstNet has met its duties and obligations under the act.[94]

A total of 34 MHz of spectrum capacity will therefore be available for public safety networks within the 700 MHz band: the 22 MHz designated for broadband, and 12 MHz allocated for narrowband communications, primarily voice.[95] Additionally, there are public safety networks on adjacent frequencies within the 800 MHz band. Time and technological advances may someday bring these spectrum assets together, but at present there are three distinct public safety network technologies in use or planned within the 700 MHz and 800 MHz bands. These are broadband communications at 700 MHz; interoperable narrowband communications at 700 MHz; and narrowband communications at 800 MHz. Some of the narrowband networks at 700 MHz and 800 MHz can share infrastructure and radios but older narrowband networks at 800 MHz are often not easily integrated with narrowband networks being built on 700 MHz frequencies.

All of the 700 MHz band spectrum allocated for public safety use can support broadband networks. At present, however, there is no tested technology to deliver voice communications over LTE broadband that meets first responder requirements. New technology that provides pushto-talk voice connections over LTE is likely to be available by the end of 2016.[96] The act also gives the FCC the authority to "... allow the narrowband spectrum to be used in a flexible manner, including usage for public safety broadband communications....” subject to technical and interference protection measures.[97] States, therefore, might be able to convert some existing narrowband networks to broadband use in addition to service from FirstNet.

The act requires that public safety users return frequencies known as the T-Band.[98] These are frequencies between 470 and 512 MHz allocated for television that have been made available for public safety use in 11 urban areas.[99] Since the transition to digital television, radio transmissions on some of these frequency assignments have experienced interference and the public safety agencies that use them are considering moving to new networks at 700 MHz. Other areas have recently invested to upgrade networks built on the T-Band frequencies and are concerned about the loss of this communications capacity. The act requires that the FCC act by February 2021 to establish a relocation plan that would free up the T-Band for reassignment through competitive bidding. Proceeds from the auctions of T-Band frequencies are to be available for grants to cover relocation costs.[100] There are no requirements in the law as to how the NTIA, the designated grants administrator, is to structure the grant program or determine eligible costs, although the agency might decide to follow procedures for reallocating federal spectrum.

Some of the earliest spectrum assignments for public safety are in channels below 512 MHz. Public safety and other license-holders in designated channels below 512 MHz are required to reband their holdings to conform to an FCC mandate to improve spectrum efficiency.[101] This narrowbanding requirement, as it is called, requires that assigned channels be reduced from a width of 25 khz to 12.5 khz, thereby freeing up new spectrum capacity for public safety and other uses. The deadline to meet the narrowbanding requirement was January 1, 2013. To accommodate public safety license holders in the T-Band that now fall under requirements established in the act, the FCC has ruled to exempt them from the narrowbanding requirements.[102]

Expenditures and Revenue Sources

The cost of building a new wireless communications network with nationwide coverage is likely to be in the tens of billions of dollars.[103] Most of these costs are for building, maintaining, and operating the Radio Access Network (RAN). To meet these costs, the expectation is that FirstNet will have access to existing infrastructure for some of the network’s components and that it will be able to invest through partnerships—with commercial wireless carriers or other secondary users of its spectrum and infrastructure—that generate revenue. However, building and operating essential elements of the core services of the network (Evolved Packet Core) are estimated by industry experts to be in the low millions of dollars.[104]

The Spectrum Act provides over $7 billion in funding directed to FirstNet and to states, either as direct transfers or as grants. There was an initial loan of $2 billion (repayable from spectrum-license auction proceeds) to set up FirstNet and begin its operation.[105] The remaining $5 billion became available as auctions for spectrum licenses were concluded and the revenues deposited in the Public Safety Trust Fund. The full amount of the federal funding commitment has been covered by auction revenue.

Public Safety Trust Fund

The law provides for transfers from a Public Safety Trust Fund, which is established in the Treasury by the act, to receive revenues from designated auctions of spectrum licenses.[106] The designated amounts are to remain available through FY2022, after which any remaining funds are to revert to the Treasury, to be used for deficit reduction. Auction proceeds are to be distributed in the following order of priority:

- To the NTIA, to reimburse the Treasury for funds advanced to cover the initial costs of establishing FirstNet: not to exceed $2 billion.
- To the State and Local Implementation Fund for a grant program: $135 million.
- To the Network Construction Fund for costs associated with building the nationwide network and for grants to states that qualify to build their own networks: $7 billion, reduced by the amount advanced to establish FirstNet.
- To NIST for public safety research: $100 million.
- To the Treasury for deficit reduction: $20.4 billion.
- To the NTIA and the National Highway Traffic Safety Administration for a grant program to improve 911 services: $115 million.
- To NIST for public safety research, phase two: $200 million.
- To the Treasury for deficit reduction: any remaining amounts from designated auction revenues.

In compliance with the act, the FCC conducted two auctions in 2014-2015 (Auctions 96 and 97) that generated sufficient revenue to meet the funding requirements of the act summarized above.[107]

FirstNet: Limit on Expenditures

The act caps FirstNet's administrative expenses at $100 million in total over the first 10 years of operation. Costs attributed to oversight and audits are not included in the expense cap.[108]

FirstNet: Fee Income and Other Revenue

Congress gave FirstNet the authority to obtain grants, and to receive payment for the use of network capacity licensed to FirstNet and of network infrastructure "constructed, owned, or operated" by FirstNet.[109] Specifically, FirstNet is authorized to collect network user fees from public safety and secondary users[110] and to receive payments under leasing agreements in public-private partnerships.[111] These partnerships may be formed between FirstNet and a secondary user for the purpose of constructing, managing, and operating the network. The agreements may allow access to the network on a secondary basis for services other than public safety.[112] The act requires that these fees be sufficient each year to cover annual expenses of FirstNet to carry out required activities,[113] with any remaining revenue going to network construction, operation, maintenance, and improvement.[114] There is a prohibition on providing service directly to consumers; this does not impact the right to collect fees from a secondary user or enter into leasing agreements.[115]

Planning Authority

The Spectrum Act created FirstNet as an independent entity within the NTIA. FirstNet is required to plan for and establish an interoperable broadband network for public safety. The act requires that state and local agencies and tribal authorities have a consulting role in the development, deployment, and operation of the nationwide network. The act further provides an opportunity for states to plan and build their own Radio Access Networks within the framework of the nationwide broadband network.[116] Unless renewed, this authority expires in 2027.[117]

When Congress creates an independent entity within the federal government, it may have the obligation to achieve a specific goal, usually within a specific time frame.[118] As an independent entity, FirstNet—the First Responder Network Authority—has been given both goals and timeframes. It has been instructed by Congress to exercise all powers specifically granted by the act and "such incidental powers as shall be necessary"[119] to create a nationwide broadband network for public safety. The law requires FirstNet to become a self-funding entity, independent of government subsidies.[120] FirstNet is to take "all actions necessary to ensure the building, deployment, and operation" of the network in consultation with federal, state, tribal, and local public safety entities, the Director of NIST, the FCC, and the public safety advisory committee.[121] FirstNet appears therefore to be an autonomous organization, with broad powers to carry out its mandate, within the requirements established by the law. It has, for example, sole power to select the program's manager and its agents, consultants, and other experts subject to the requirement that they be chosen "in a fair, transparent, and objective manner."[122] However, FirstNet, except for certain exemptions provided in the act, must follow federal agency requirements, notably in hiring and procurement, slowing down the process for establishing FirstNet as a going concern.[123]

FirstNet is headed by a board of 15 members of which 12 are appointed by the Secretary of Commerce according to criteria established by the act, which are intended to provide both representation from key stakeholders and expertise. The other three members of the board are designees of the Secretary of the Department of Homeland Security, the Attorney General of the United States, and the Director of the Office of Management and Budget. The Secretary of Commerce is required to appoint a chairman of the board for an initial term of two years.[124]

As part of its management of the network, FirstNet is required, at a minimum:

- To establish network policies, including development of detailed requests for proposals to build the network, and operational matters such as terms of service and billing practices.[125]
- To consult with states on network-related expenditures, as part of the preparation of policies and requests for proposals.[126]
- To enter into agreements to use existing communications infrastructure, including commercial and federal infrastructure, "to the maximum extent economically desirable."[127]
- To ensure the construction, maintenance, operation, and improvement of the broadband network, taking into account new and evolving technologies.[128]

- To enter into agreements with commercial networks to allow public safety roaming on their networks.[129]
- To represent the interests of the network's users before standards-setting boards, in consultation with NIST, the FCC, and its own Public Safety Advisory Committee.[130]

FirstNet is required to create a public safety advisory committee to assist in carrying out its mandate.[131] There are no requirements in the statute as to the composition of the committee. Bylaws adopted at the organizing meeting of the FirstNet Board of Directors on September 25, 2012, created a Public Safety Advisory Committee.[132] It was further agreed that the members of the committee would be chosen from the Advisory Committee to SAFECOM, within the Department of Homeland Security, in consultation with the Secretary of Homeland Security. The organizations chosen to be represented on the committee were announced on February 20, 2013.[133] State and local government interests are represented through a subcommittee of PSAC.

Statutory Obligations

Examples of statutory obligations for Congress and the Administration in the direction of FirstNet include the following.

Membership on FirstNet board. The members of the FirstNet board are to be chosen by the Secretary of Commerce, within the parameters established in the act. The Department of Homeland Security, the Attorney General, and the Office of Management and Budget each have one member on the board in permanence. The Secretary of Commerce is required to appoint a chairman of the board for an initial term of two years.[134]

Grant programs for planning. The NTIA is to establish and administer the State and Local Implementation Fund. Grant provisions are to be decided in consultation with FirstNet,[135] but not necessarily in accordance with decisions made by the FirstNet board and executive management.

Grant programs for state networks. The NTIA is to administer grants from the Network Construction Fund to states that qualify to build their own Radio Access Networks and choose to apply for a grant.[136]

Funding for FirstNet and participating states through the Network Construction Fund. The NTIA is to determine the funding level available to each state for the buildout of the nationwide broadband network, if the state chooses to participate in FirstNet.[137]

Spectrum leases for state networks. The NTIA sets the terms and is responsible for enforcing the requirement that states qualifying to build their Radio Access Networks must sublease spectrum through FirstNet, the assigned license-holder.[138]

License review. The FCC is required to review the initial 10-year license assigned to FirstNet and consider its renewal based on performance criteria.[139]

Performance review. The Government Accountability Office (GAO), within 10 years, is to prepare a report providing recommendations on "what action Congress should take" regarding the mandated termination of authority of FirstNet in 2027.[140]

Fee schedule. The NTIA is to review and approve the annual schedule of fees charged to public safety agencies and other users for access to FirstNet's resources.[141]

Annual audit. The Secretary of Commerce is to contract for an annual audit of FirstNet's finances and activities. The reports are to be submitted to Congress, the President, and FirstNet.[142]

Report to Congress. FirstNet is required to submit annual reports to Congress on its "operations, activities, financial conditions, and accomplishments."[143] The designated appropriate congressional committees are, in the Senate, the Committee on Commerce, Science, and Transportation; in the House, the Committee on Energy and Commerce.[144]

Although there are several platforms for oversight and guidance provided in the act, it seems likely that the primary, day-to-day responsibility for monitoring progress will fall to the NTIA. Agency discretion for funding states that participate in FirstNet and for providing grants to states that opt out is authorized by the act. The $7 billion grant to the Network Construction Fund is implicitly divided into three parts: one funding FirstNet to establish the network; one funding states that participate in FirstNet; and one funding states that choose to opt out. Clauses that may have been intended to oversee state expenditures might be construed by the NTIA to include FirstNet. The act, however, does not provide guidance to the NTIA on how to balance fiduciary caution with entrepreneurial initiative in assuring a flow of funds to FirstNet.

Public-Private Partnerships

Partnerships are expected to play a critical role in building and operating the network. Electric utility companies, for example, might benefit from a partnership that helped to upgrade their networks to meet Smart Grid requirements.[145] Some commercial wireless service providers have also expressed an interest in working in partnership with public safety entities to develop and operate new broadband networks.

The Spectrum Act requires FirstNet to issue "open, transparent, and competitive" requests for proposals to private sector entities for building, operating, and maintaining the network[146] that leverage to the extent "economically desirable" existing commercial wireless infrastructure, in order to expedite network deployment.[147] It is charged with managing and overseeing the resulting contracts or agreements. As part of a separate requirement to assure substantial rural coverage during all phases of deployment, the act requires that industry proposals and contracts include, if possible, partnerships with existing commercial mobile providers.[148]

Decisions by FirstNet about the network's design, construction, and operation are likely to have a significant impact on commercial participation in a public safety broadband network or networks. These decisions may also influence decision-making by states as to whether or not to pursue radio area network construction independently or through their own partnerships.

Infrastructure

Infrastructure for the new network includes operations centers, towers, antennae, base stations, routers, small cell nodes, and other communications equipment, as well as radios and the software that links them to the network. For wireless communications, an important infrastructure component is the connection between base stations and communications backbones. These networks, which usually operate over fiber-optic cable or microwave connection, are typically referred to as backhaul.

The Spectrum Act requires FirstNet to establish a nationwide, interoperable public safety network.[149] Network infrastructure components that are specifically required include

- Core network of national and regional data centers and other elements, all based on commercial standards.
- Connectivity between the Radio Access Network and the public Internet or the Public Switched Telephone Network, or both.
- Network cell site equipment, antennas, and backhaul equipment, based on commercial standards, to support wireless devices operating on frequencies designated for public safety broadband.[150]

FirstNet is required to leverage existing infrastructure by entering into agreements to use commercial or other communications infrastructure, including federal, state, tribal, or local infrastructure.[151] Planned phases for infrastructure deployment are to include "substantial rural coverage."[152]

FirstNet's ability to build the required network may depend on the timeliness, scope, and outcome of its negotiations to share infrastructure with other parties in order to focus resources on providing elements deemed essential for public safety use of broadband communications.

Timeframe

The requirements of the Spectrum Act must be substantially met and the viability of the project demonstrated no later than the end of FY2022, if not sooner. The State and Local Implementation Fund and the Network Construction Fund expire in 2022, with any balances reverting to the Treasury. By 2022, GAO must have assessed the performance of FirstNet and provided a report to Congress; and the FCC must decide whether or not to renew the licenses for the public safety broadband network. Within this 10-year timeframe, there are few deadlines beyond requirements for the initial establishment of the planning and implementation framework.

Many of the important steps for building the network have no required deadline. Some milestones, such as rural coverage, are mandated in the act, but the deadlines are not specified. There are, for example, no deadlines in provisions that require FirstNet to:

- Develop requests for proposals that include a requirement for timetables.[153]
- Consult with states on establishing state and local planning processes.[154]
- Complete the request for proposal process that is to be given to each state governor regarding the request for proposal and its details, and the funding level for each state as determined by the NTIA.[155]

Mandated deadlines for states include

- Within 90 days of receipt of notice from FirstNet, the governor shall choose either to participate in deployment of FirstNet or to conduct its own Radio Access Network deployment within the state.[156]

- Within 180 days of giving notice to opt out of FirstNet, the governor shall complete requests for proposals for a state network.[157]

No deadline is established in the statute for the FCC to approve or disapprove state proposals for their own portion of the nationwide broadband network.[158] There are also no specified deadlines for a state to apply to the NTIA for a grant to construct the Radio Access Network and to lease spectrum capacity from FirstNet, if FCC approval is received for a state network.[159] However, one condition of eligibility for a grant to a state to build its own Radio Access Network is that the state's plan must demonstrate "the ability to complete the project within specified comparable deadlines...."[160]

Next Generation 9-1-1

Today's 911 system is built on an infrastructure of analog technology that does not support many of the features that most Americans expect to be part of an emergency response. Efforts to splice newer, digital technologies onto this aging infrastructure have created points of failure where a call can be dropped or misdirected, sometimes with tragic consequences. Callers to 911, however, generally assume that the newer technologies they are using to place a call are matched by the same level of technology at the 911 call centers, known as Public Safety Answering Points (PSAPs). However, this is not always the case. To modernize the system to provide the quality of service that approaches the expectations of its users will require that the PSAPs and state, local, and possibly federal emergency communications authorities invest in new technologies. As envisioned by most stakeholders, these new technologies—collectively referred to as Next Generation 911 or NG9-1-1—should incorporate Internet Protocol standards. An IP-enabled emergency communications network that supports 911 will facilitate interoperability and system resilience; improve connections between 911 call centers; provide more robust capacity; and offer flexibility in receiving and managing calls. The same network can also serve wireless broadband communications for public safety and other emergency personnel, as well as other purposes.

Recognizing the importance of providing effective 911 service, Congress has previously passed three major bills supporting improvements in the handling of 911 emergency calls. The Wireless Communications and Public Safety Act of 1999 (P.L. 106-81) established 911 as the number to call for emergencies and gave the Federal Communications Commission (FCC) authority to regulate many aspects of the service. The most recent of these laws, the NET 911 Improvement Act of 2008 (P.L. 110-283), required the preparation of a National Plan for migrating to an IPenabled emergency network. Responsibility for the plan was assigned to the E-911 Implementation Coordination Office (ICO), created to meet requirements of an earlier law, the ENHANCE 911 Act of 2004 (P.L. 108-494). Authorization for the ICO terminated on September 30, 2009. ICO was jointly administered by the National Telecommunications and Information Administration and the National Highway Traffic Safety Administration.

Spectrum Act provisions re-establish the federal 9-1-1 Implementation Coordination Office (ICO) to advance planning for next-generation systems and to administer a grant program.[161] ICO is to provide matching grants to eligible state or local governments or tribal organizations for the implementation, operation, and migration of various types of 911 and IP-enabled emergency services, and for public safety personnel training.[162] States that have diverted fees collected for 911 services are not eligible for grants under the program.[163]

Provisions in the act regarding 911 programs include

- GAO is required to study how states assess fees on 911 services and how those fees are used.[164]
- The General Services Administration is required to prepare a report on 911 capabilities of multi-line telephone systems in federal facilities and the FCC is to seek comment on the feasibility of improving 911 identification for calls placed through multi-line telephone systems.[165]
- The FCC is to assess the legal and regulatory environment for development of NG9-1-1 and barriers to that development, including state regulatory roadblocks.[166] The FCC is also to (1) initiate a proceeding to create a specialized Do-Not-Call registry for public safety answering points, and (2) to establish penalties and fines for autodialing (robocalls) and related violations.[167]
- ICO, in consultation with NHTSA and DHS is to report on costs for requirements and specifications of NG9-1-1 services, including an analysis of costs, and assessments and analyses of technical uses.[168]
- Immunity and liability protections are provided—to the extent consistent with specified provisions of the Wireless Communications and Public Safety Act of 1999—for various users and providers of Next Generation 911 and related services, including for the release of subscriber information.[169]

The act also requires FirstNet to promote integration of the nationwide public safety broadband network with PSAPs.[170] Draft proposals consider PSAPs as customers of FirstNet[171] but do not specifically discuss the integration of NG-9-1-1 infrastructure into the FirstNet network.

Roaming and Priority Access within the 700 MHz Band

In its *National Broadband Plan*, the FCC indicated that it wanted to make commercial networks in the 700 MHz band available for public safety use and requested that Congress confirm the FCC's authority to act.[172] The Spectrum Act provides the FCC with statutory authority to establish rules in the public interest to improve the ability of public safety networks to roam on commercial space and to gain priority access.[173]

FirstNet is empowered by the act to enter into agreements with commercial providers that would allow public safety network users to roam on partnering networks.[174] The act does not state whether roaming agreements may be negotiated by states that opt out and receive spectrum leases from the NTIA to operate their own Radio Access networks. Agreements might also cover rules for priority access in times of high demand for network capacity. Priority access can take several forms, such as "ruthless pre-emption," in which non-public-safety transmissions are immediately terminated to make way for emergency communications, or negotiated priority agreements that might, for example, place public safety users at the head of the line for network access as capacity becomes available. The act stipulates that the FCC's authority may not require roaming or priority access unless (1) the public safety and commercial networks are technically compatible; (2) the commercial network is reasonably compensated; and (3) access does not preempt or otherwise terminate or degrade existing traffic on the commercial network.[175] Within these limits, the FCC appears to have some leeway to use its regulatory authority to support public safety in negotiations with partners. The FCC cannot, under the act, mandate ruthless pre-emption, although the act does not preclude contractual negotiations that would allow it.

The act's provisions for roaming and priority access do not require a commercial vendor to make additional investments to insure technical compatibility, and the act's language might be interpreted as precluding an FCC mandate to that effect. Interpretation and enforcement of the compatibility provision may pose an obstacle to achieving desired levels of network interoperability and cross-network roaming because existing technical standards for the 700 MHz band might preclude affordable full-spectrum roaming, that is, the ability of any network within the 700 MHz to roam on any other network within the 700 MHz band. Full-spectrum roaming is considered by many to provide advantages for public safety and also for the public at large. For example, it makes more network capacity available for shared emergency communications of all types, not just for first responders. Many believe that full-spectrum access supports competitiveness among wireless carriers—in particular assisting small wireless carriers serving rural areas to offer new broadband services—by providing access to all customers within the band.

Achieving full-spectrum roaming on the 700 MHz band requires modifications of technical requirements for LTE, the preferred technology for mobile broadband within the 700 MHz band. The FCC has taken actions in support of full-spectrum roaming,[176] including steps to implement a voluntary industry agreement to establish interoperability for LTE in the lower 700 MHz band.[177] Establishing additional standards to enable full-spectrum interoperability will permit interoperability among all commercial carriers and public safety agencies.

End Notes

[1] P.L. 112-96, Section 6204 (a).

[2] P.L. 112-96, Section 6202 (b) (2) (B).

[3] The spectrum license issued to FirstNet is for two 10 MHz channels of paired spectrum at 758-768 MHz and 788-798 MHz, plus guard bands at 768-769 MHz and 798-799 MHz to mitigate interference from adjacent channels. For purposes of allocation and assignment, spectrum is segmented into bands of radio frequencies measured in cycles per second, or hertz. Standard abbreviations for measuring frequencies include kHz—kilohertz or thousands of hertz; MHz—megahertz, or millions of hertz; and GHz—gigahertz, or billions of hertz. The designation can refer to an entire band, such as the 700 MHz band, or to specific frequencies within a band.

[4] Summaries of these agency reports appear in later sections of this report.

[5] FirstNet, Request for Information for Comprehensive Network Solution(s), September 17, 2014, http://www.firstnet.gov/sites/default /files/Request%20for%20Information% 20for% 20Comprehensive%20Network%20Solutions.pdf.

[6] Congressional Research Service was informed of the outline for FirstNet's comprehensive network strategy in discussion with NTIA officials between July and September 2012.

[7] FirstNet, Second Notice, March 9, 2015, at http://www.firstnet.gov/sites/default/files/ FirstNet_Second_Public_Notice_0.pdfplus; also published in Federal Register, Vol. 80, No. 49, Friday, March 13, 2015, 1336-13351 (Docket Number 150306226-5226-01); comments due by April 28, 2015.

[8] FirstNet, Public Notice on Statutory Interpretations, September 17, 2014, at http://www.firstnet.gov/sites/default/ files/firstnet-public-notice-middle-class-tax-relief-job-creation-act-of-2012.pdf.

[9] FirstNet, "Further Proposed Interpretations of Parts of the Middle Class Tax Relief and Job Creation Act of 2012," at http://www.firstnet.gov/sites/default/files/firstnet-third-notice-final-prepublication-version.pdf.

[10] FirstNet, Special Board Meeting Agenda, http://www.firstnet.gov/sites/default/files/FirstNet-April-24-2015-MeetingAgenda.pdf

[11] "FirstNet's Proposed Acquisition Approach," April 24, 2015, at http://www.firstnet.gov/sites/ default/files/firstnetspecial-notice-and-draft-rfp-documents_0.pdf.

[12] FirstNet, Special Notice and supporting documents for draft RFP, Federal Business Opportunities, Solicitation Number D15PS00295, at https://www.fbo.gov/index?s= opportunity&mode=form&tab=core&id= 55fa4d3227d5ac0173e4613e04368c86.

[13] As a federal agency, FirstNet is required to follow federal procurement processes but the act does not mandate the use of FAR. Some legal experts might argue that the contracts to be negotiated through the RFP process are not subject to FAR. For more information on FAR, see CRS Report R42826, The Federal Acquisition Regulation (FAR): Answers to Frequently Asked Questions, by Kate M. Manuel et al.

[14] FirstNet, Special Notice, op. cit.

[15] Fact Sheet, "FirstNet and Federal Departments and Agencies," October 2014 at http://www. firstnet.gov/sites/default/ files/federal-information-fact-sheet-1.pdf.

[16] Ibid.

[17] Ibid.

[18] FirstNet, Request for Information for Comprehensive Network Solution(s), September 17, 2014, http://www.firstnet.gov/sites/default/files/Request%20for%20Information%20for%20Comprehensive%20Network%20Solutions.pdf.

[19] "We believe as a general matter that Congress did not intend for a few, high density states to be able to withhold material funding for all the other States under the Act." Second Notice, op.cit.

[20] FirstNet, Special Notice: Statement of Objectives, C.3, "Program Descriptions." April 27, 2015.

[21] FirstNet, Special Notice, 4.3, "FirstNet's Proposed Approaches—Prior to State RAN Decision," April 27, 2015.

[22] FirstNet, Special Notice: Statement of Objectives, C.3, "Program Descriptions," April 27, 2015.

[23] Department of Homeland Security, National Emergency Communications Plan, November 12, 2014, p .7: "... the primary means to achieve mission critical voice communications." At http://www.dhs.gov/sites/default/files/publications/2014%20National%20Emergency%20Communications%20Plan_October%2029%202014.pdf.

[24] The California Bay Area Regional Interoperable Communications Systems Authority is testing a wireless broadband network for public safety developed by xG Technology that can be deployed on existing LMR infrastructure.

[25] "FirstNet LTE Overview," at http://www.firstnet.gov/sites/default/files/LTE%20Overview-.pdf. The version referenced in this report is dated March 2, 2015.

[26] Small cells are low-powered radio access nodes that are used to boost capacity and manage network interference and connectivity. The types of small cells include Femtocells, typically used in a home; Picocells, that may serve a business; Metrocells, for urban areas; and Microcells, the largest in terms of geographic coverage, used primarily in rural areas.

The term small cells is used by the Small Cell Forum as an umbrella term for operator-controlled, low-power radio access nodes using licensed or unlicensed spectrum.

[27] A more detailed discussion of the evolution of wireless network concepts appears in CRS Report R43595, Mobile Technology and Spectrum Policy: Innovation and Competition, by Linda K. Moore.

[28] P.L. 112-96, Sec. 6202 (b) states that the network consists of "(1) a core network that—(A) consists of national and regional data centers, and other elements that may be distributed geographically, all of which shall be based on commercial standards; and (B) provides the connectivity between—(i) the radio access network; and (ii) the public Internet and the public switched network, or both; and (2) a radio access network that—(A) consists of all cell site equipment, antennas, and backhaul equipment, based on commercial standards, that are required to enable wireless communications, with devices using the public safety broadband spectrum; and (B) shall be developed, constructed, managed, maintained, and operated taking into account the State, local, and tribal planning and implementation grant program, under section 6302 (a)."

[29] In 2012, small cell deployments now commonly used by the industry to expand their LTE networks were considered experimental, for example comments in President's Council of Advisors on Science and Technology (PCAST), Realizing the Full Potential of Government-Held Spectrum to Spur Economic Growth, July 20, 2012, at https://www.whitehouse.gov/sites/default/files/microsites/ostp/pcast_spectrum_report_final_july_20_2012.pdf.

[29] FirstNet, Second Notice, at http://www.firstnet.gov/sites/default/files/FirstNet_Second_Public_Notice_0.pdfplus.

[30] The discussion is based on currently available information as of the publication date of this report.

[31] CRS meeting with FirstNet officials, February 13, 2015.

[32] FirstNet, Public Notice on Statutory Interpretations, at http://www.firstnet.gov/sites/default/files/firstnet-publicnotice-middle-class-tax-relief-job-creation-act-of-2012.pdf. The Special Notice, "Terms of Reference," reiterates the proposed definition but does not provide a conclusive description of RAN.

[33] CRS meeting with FirstNet officials, February 13, 2015.

[34] Ibid.

[35] Hearing, Senate Committee on Commerce, Science, and Transportation, "Three Years Later: Are We Any Closer to a Nationwide Public Safety Network," March 11, 2015: oral testimony of Ms. Susan Swenson, Chairwoman, FirstNet. Ms. Swenson further explained that FirstNet had found it difficult to negotiate for access to state and local infrastructure as part of its pilot with the Los Angeles Regional Interoperable Communications System (LA-RICS). See also FirstNet, "Early Builder's Blog, February12, 2015, at http://www.firstnet.gov/newsroom/blog/early-builders-blogla-rics.

[36] Ibid.

[37] FirstNet, Second Notice, at http://www.firstnet.gov/sites/default/files/FirstNet_Second_Public_Notice_0.pdfplus.

[38] This phrase has reportedly been used in many discussions between FirstNet staff and Members of Congress or their staff. It was also used in the February 13, 2015 CRS meeting with FirstNet officials.

[39] Examples of sources that discuss potential value or wireless broadband for rural, suburban, and urban areas include Small Cell Forum case studies, including rural and remote areas (http://scf.io/en/documents/047_Extending_rural_and_remote_coverage_using_small_cells.

php); NTIA, Broadband USA: An Introduction to Effective Public-Private Partnerships for Broadband Investments (http://scf.io/en/documents/ 047_Extending_rural_and_remote_coverage_using_small_cells.php);and testimony at Senate and House hearings on the Internet of Things (Senate, Committee on Commerce, Science, and Transportation, February 11, 2015; House, Committee on Energy and Commerce, March 24, 2015).

[40] FCC News, "FCC Announces Wireless Spectrum Cap to Sunset Effective January 1, 2003," November 8, 2001. Report and Order FCC-01-328. See Docket No. 01-14, Notice of Proposed Rulemaking, released January 23, 2001, at http://hraunfoss.fcc.gov/edocs_public/attachmatch/FCC-01-28A1.pdf.

[41] FirstNet, "Stakeholder Quarterly Webinar," April 2, 2015, presentation on FirstNet Second Notice by Eli Veenendaal, Attorney-Advisor, at http://www.firstnet.gov/sites/default/files/Stakeholder_Qtrly_Webinar_20150402.pdf.

[42] See, for example, Qualcomm, "1000x: More Small Cells; Hyper-Dense Small Cell Deployments," June 2014. For presentation slides, see http://www.slideshare.net/qualcommwirelessevolution/web-bringing-1000x-closer-to-realityhyper-dense-small-cells-wirelessnetworks-052014.

[43] See, for example, Computerworld, "Verizon Boosts Role in Farm Services and Smart Cities," by Matt Hamblen, May 1, 2015, at http://www.computerworld.com/article/2917932/internet-of-things/verizon-boosts-role-in-smart-citiesand-farms-services.html.

[44] The act requires FirstNet to reinvest in the network any excess receipts from the fees it is authorized to collect, P.L. 112-96, Section 6207 (b).

[45] These advantages were, for example, highlighted in presentations at FirstNet's "Stakeholder Quarterly Webinar," April 2, 2015 (http://www.firstnet.gov/sites/default/files/Stakeholder Qtrly_Webinar_20150402.pdf) as well as in other documents.

[46] See "Statewide Interoperability Coordinators," at http://www.dhs.gov/files/programs/gc_1286986920144.shtm.

[47] P.L. 112-96, Section 6206 (c) (2) (B).

[48] P.L. 112-96, Section 6302 (d).

[49] Hearing, House Committee on Energy and Commerce, Subcommittee on Communications and Technology, "Oversight of FirstNet and the Advancement of Public Safety Wireless Communications," testimony of Samuel Ginn, Chairman, FirstNet, November 21, 2013. List of state contacts at http://www.firstnet.gov/sites/default/files/spoc-listdirectory-20150113.pdf.

[50] P.L. 112-96, Section 6302 (e) (1).

[51] A discussion of courses a state might choose appears in a blog post on medium com: Bill Schrier, "FirstNet: More Choices than Just Opt-In/out," February 7, 2015, https://medium.com/@BillSchrier/firstnet-more-choices-than-just-optin-out-cb47b306b62c.

[52] FirstNet, Second Notice, at http://www.firstnet.gov/sites/default/files/FirstNet_ Second_Public_Notice_0.pdfplus.

[53] P.L. 112-96, Section 6302 (e) (2) and (3).

[54] P.L. 112-96, Section 6302 (e) (3) (D).

[55] P.L. 112-96, Section 6302 (f).

[56] P.L. 112-96, Section 6302 (g).

[57] P.L. 112-96, Section 6413.

[58] NTIA Press Releases, "NTIA Announces Second Phase of Funding for State and Local Implementation Grant Program," March 23, 2015, http://www.ntia.doc.gov/press-release/2015/ntia-announces-second-phase-funding-stateand-local-implementation-grant-program.

[59] Bill Schrier, the Chief Seattle Geek Blog, "Live Long and Prosper: Impressions from the SPOCs Meeting," April 19, 2015, at https://schrier.wordpress.com/2015/04/19/live-long-and-prosper-impressions-from-the-spocs-meeting/.

[60] P.L. 112-96, Section 6413.

[61] P.L. 112-96, Section 6206 (e).

[62] FirstNet, Special Notice, "4.5 Proposed Pricing Methodology" proposes two main elements: "Level of Government Funding," quoted above; and "level of Fixed Payments to FirstNet," regarding fixed payments to FirstNet.

[63] FirstNet, U.S. Department of Commerce, FY2014: Annual Report to Congress, at http://www.firstnet.gov/sites/ default/files/Annual%20Report_FY2014_FINAL_3_3_15.pdf.

[64] FirstNet News, "FirstNet Finance Committee Gives Go-Ahead to Fund Key RFP, Consultation Activities in FY15," November 17, 2015, at http://www.firstnet.gov/news/ firstnet-finance-committee-gives-go-ahead-fund-key-rfpconsultation-activities-fy15.

[65] Hearing, Senate Committee on Commerce, Science, and Transportation, "Three Years Later: Are We Any Closer to a Nationwide Public Safety Network," March 11, 2015: testimony of The Honorable Todd J. Zinser, Inspector General, U.S. Department of Commerce at http://www.commerce.senate.gov/public/index.cfm?p=Hearings& ContentRecord_id=25dedd7c-815b-4b3d-a420-4f4324d01041&Statement_id=ec8d2396-ecd6-4787-bcc6-6c0152203066&ContentType_id=14f995b9-dfa5-407a-9d35-56cc7 152a7ed&Group_id=b06c39af-e033-4cba-9221-de668ca1978a&MonthDisplay=3&YearDisplay=2015.

[66] U.S. Department of Commerce, National Telecommunications and Information Administration, FY 2016 Budget as Presented to Congress, February 2015, at http://www.ntia.doc.gov/files/ntia/publications/ntia_2016_cj_final_2-5-15- 508_checked.pdf.

[67] Hearing, Senate Committee on Commerce, Science, and Transportation, "Three Years Later: Are We Any Closer to a Nationwide Public Safety Network," March 11, 2015: Testimony of Mark L. Goldstein, Director, Physical Infrastructure Issues, GAO at http://www.commerce.senate.gov/public/?a=Files.Serve&File_id=782a6761-b54b-4e6b918d-6bd28b287f34.

[68] GAO, Public-Safety Broadband Network: FirstNet Should Strengthen Internal Controls and Evaluate Lessons Learned, GAO-15-407, April 2015, at http://www.gao.gov/assets/ 670/669861.pdf.

[69] The early builder projects refer to four recipients of BTOP (Broadband Technology Opportunities Program) grants from the NTIA that also qualified for temporary sub-leases of the spectrum license held by FirstNet as well as Harris County, TX, which qualified for a license but did not receive a BTOP grant. These programs are intended to provide valuable lessons for FirstNet as it prepares to deploy nationwide. The four early builders with BTOP grants are Los Angeles County, CA (LA-RICS); Adams County, CO; New Jersey; and New Mexico. Three recipients with BTOP grants that did not qualify as early builders are Charlotte, NC; San Francisco, CA; and Mississippi. More information regarding the early builders is on the FirstNet website and in its FY2014 Annual Report to Congress. Information on BTOP grant programs appears in CRS Report R41775, Background and Issues for Congressional Oversight of ARRA Broadband Awards, by Lennard G. Kruger.

[70] GAO, Public-Safety Broadband Network: FirstNet Should Strengthen Internal Controls and Evaluate Lessons Learned, GAO-15-407, April 2015, p. 32, at http://www.gao.gov/ assets/670/669861.pdf.

[71] OIG, First Responder Network Authority: FirstNet Must Strengthen Management of Financial Disclosures and Monitoring of Contracts, Final Report No. OIG-15-013-A, December 5, 2014, at http://www.oig.doc.gov/ OIGPublications/OIG-15-013-A.pdf.

[72] Ibid., cover memorandum.

[73] Ibid., p. 36.

[74] Ibid., p. 5.

[75] Ibid., p. 6.

[76] Ibid., p. 12.

[77] Hearing, Senate Committee on Commerce, Science, and Transportation, "Three Years Later: Are We Any Closer to a Nationwide Public Safety Network," March 11, 2015: testimony of The Honorable Todd J. Zinser, Inspector General, U.S. Department of Commerce at http://www.commerce.senate.gov/public/index.cfm?p=Hearings& ContentRecord_id=25dedd7c-815b-4b3d-a420-4f4324d01041&Statement_id=ec8d2396-ecd6-4787-bcc6- 6c0152203066&ContentType_id=14f995b9-dfa5-407a-9d35-56cc7152a7ed&Group_id=b06c39af-e033-4cba-9221-de668ca1978a&MonthDisplay= 3&YearDisplay=2015.

[78] Hearing, House Committee on Energy and Commerce, Subcommittee on Communications and Technology, "Oversight of FirstNet and the Advancement of Public Safety Wireless Communications," testimony of Samuel Ginn, Chairman, FirstNet, November 21, 2013.

[79] "FirstNet Program Roadmap Executive Summary," at http://firstnet.gov/sites/default/files/ FirstNet%20Program%20Roadmap%20Executive%20Summary_03112014.pdf.

[80] FirstNet News, "FirstNet Board of Directors Meets on Strategic Roadmap," March 11, 2014, http://www.firstnet.gov/ news/firstnet-board-directors-meets-strategic-roadmap.

[81] According to information supplied by the NTIA to CRS on January 12, 2015, FirstNet is conducting consultations that are broader than just the states and the Roadmap has been modified to reflect this action.

[82] FurstNet News, "FirstNet Moves Forward on Strategic Program Roadmap in Open Board Meeting," June 3, 2014, http://www.firstnet.gov/news/firstnet-moves-forward-strategic-program-roadmap-open-board-meeting.

[83] Board Resolution 1, By-Laws, http://www.ntia.doc.gov/files/ntia/publications/ firstnet_ resolution_no._1_on_bylaws_adopted_9.25.12.pdf.

[84] FirstNet News, "FirstNet Finance Committee Gives Go-Ahead to Fund Key RFP, Consultation Activities in FY15," http://www.firstnet.gov/news/firstnet-finance-committee-gives-go-ahead-fund-key-rfp-consultation-activities-fy15.

[85] Request for Information for Comprehensive Network Solution(s), September 17, 2014, http://www.firstnet.gov/sites/default/files/Request%20for%20Information%20for% 20Comprehensive%20Network%20Solutions.pdf; posted on FedBizOpps.gov, https://www.fbo.gov/index?s=opportunity&mode=form&id= 291b788f075a 806550ca9c19955793a8&tab=core&tabmode=list&=.

[86] FirstNet News, "FirstNet Holds First State Plan Consultation Meeting Maryland," July 29, 2014, http://www.firstnet.gov/news/firstnet-holds-first-state-plan-consultation-meeting-maryland.

[87] "Strategic Roadmap Management Update," http://www.firstnet.gov/sites/default/files/firstnet-strategic-roadmapmanagement-update_0.pdf

[88] The information in this and following sections has appeared in earlier versions of this report.

[89] WiFi, for wireless fidelity, operates on unlicensed frequencies that are not assigned to a specific owner but instead are available to support any device approved by the FCC.

[90] Spectrum is segmented into bands of radio frequencies and typically measured in cycles per second, or hertz. Standard abbreviations for measuring frequencies include kHz—kilohertz or thousands of hertz; MHz—megahertz, or millions of hertz; and GHz—gigahertz, or billions of hertz. The 700 MHz band includes radio frequencies from 698 MHz to 806 MHz.

[91] 47 U.S.C. §309 (j) (14).

[92] 763-768 MHz, 793-798 MHz, 768-769 MHz and 798-799 MHz.

[93] 758-763 MHz and 788-793 MHz; P.L. 112-96, Section 6001, (2).

[94] P.L. 112-96, Section 6201.

[95] 769-775 MHz and 799-805 MHz.

[96] Push-to-talk—walkie-talkie—provides the capability for group communications. 3GPP, the international standards group for LTE, has announced that mission-critical voice communications will be available over LTE networks in 2016. See Donny Jackson, "LTE Standards Group Targeting Mission-Critical Push-to-Talk Voice Spcifications for Early 2016," Urgent Communications, February 12, 2015, http://urgentcomm.com/3gpp/lte-standards-group-targetingmission-critical-push-talk-specifications-early-2016?NL=UC-03&Issue=UC-03_20150212_UC-03_140&sfvc4enews=42&cl=article_2_b&YM_RID=CPEQW000001101112&YM_MID=2611.

[97] P.L. 112-96, Section 6102.

[98] P.L. 112-96, Section 6103.

[99] Metropolitan areas: Boston, MA; Chicago, IL; Dallas/Fort Worth, TX; Houston, TX; Los Angeles, CA; Miami, FL; New York, NY/Newark NJ; Philadelphia, PA; Pittsburgh, PA; San Francisco/Oakland, CA; and Washington, DC.

[100] The National Public Safety Telecommunications Council (NPSTC) prepared a report that provided an overview of T-Band assignments, some of the problems created by the act's requirements, and possible alternative solutions. NPSTC, T-Band Report, March 15, 2013; link to PDF at http://www.npstc.org/, "NPSTC Releases T Band Report."

[101] Details at http://transition.fcc.gov/pshs/public-safety-spectrum/narrowbanding.html.

[102] FCC, "Waiver of Narrowbanding Deadlines for T-Band (470-512 MHz) Licenses," Docket No. WT 99-87, released April 26, 2012.

[103] Some cost estimates for building and operating a public safety broadband network are provided by GAO in Preliminary Information on FirstNet's Efforts to Establish a Nationwide Broadband Network, March 11, 2015, at http://www.commerce.senate.govpublic/?a=Files.Serve&File_id=782a6761-b54b-4e6b-918d-6bd28b287f34.

[104] Elements needed for a nationwide, redundant, load-sharing network core would include the key control node (Mobility Management Entity, MME); Serving Gateway; and Packet Data Network Gateway. Source: "LTE and Beyond," January 7, 2012, at http://www.lteandbeyond.com/2012/01/functions-of-main-lte-packet-core.html.

[105] P.L. 112-96, Section 6207.

[106] P.L. 112-96, Section 6413.

[107] For additional information on the auctions, see CRS Report R43256, Spectrum Policy: Provisions in the 2012 Spectrum Act, by Linda K. Moore.

[108] P.L. 112-96, Section 6207 (b).

[109] P.L. 112-96, Section 6206 (b) (4).

[110] P.L. 112-96, Section 6208 (a) (1).

[111] P.L. 112-96, Section 6208 (a) (2).

[112] P.L. 112-96, Section 6208 (a) (2) (B).

[113] P.L. 112-96, Section 6208 (b).

[114] P.L. 112-96, Section 6208 (d).

[115] P.L. 112-96, Section 6212.
[116] Current information on FirstNet's activities, including network design and state planning, is available at http://www.firstnet.gov.
[117] P.L. 112-96, Section 6206 (f).
[118] For examples, see CRS Report RS22230, Congressional or Federal Charters: Overview and Enduring Issues, by Henry B. Hogue.
[119] P.L. 112-96, Section 6206 (a) (1).
[120] P.L. 112-96, Section 6208.
[121] P.L. 112-96, Section 6206 (b) (1).
[122] P.L. 112-96, Section 6205 (b) (1).
[123] Hearing, House Committee on Energy and Commerce, Subcommittee on Communications and Technology, "Oversight of FirstNet and the Advancement of Public Safety Wireless Communications," testimony of Samuel Ginn, Chairman, FirstNet, November 21, 2013.
[124] P.L. 112-96, Section 6204.
[125] P.L. 112-96, Section 6206 (c) (1).
[126] P.L. 112-96, Section 6206 (c) (2).
[127] P.L. 112-96, Section 6206 (c) (3).
[128] P.L. 112-96, Section 6206 (c) (4).
[129] P.L. 112-96, Section 6206 (c) (5).
[130] P.L. 112-96, Section 6206 (c) (7).
[131] P.L. 112-96, Section 6205 (a).
[132] Board Resolution 1, By-Laws, http://www.ntia.doc.gov/files/ntia/publications/firstnet_resolution_no._1_on_bylaws_adopted_9.25.12.pdf.
[133] NTIA, "FirstNet Names members of Public Safety Advisory Committee," February 20, 2013, http://www.ntia.doc.gov/press-release/2013/firstnet-names-members-public-safety-advisory-committee.
[134] P.L. 112-96, Section 6204.
[135] P.L. 112-96, Section 6302 (a).
[136] P.L. 112-96, Section 6302 (e) (3) (C) (iii) (I).
[137] P.L. 112-96, Section 6302 (e) (1) (C).
[138] P.L. 112-96, Section 6302 (e) (3) (C) (iii) (II).
[139] P.L. 112-96, Section 6201 (b).
[140] P.L. 112-96, Section 6206 (g).
[141] P.L. 112-96, Section 6208 (c).
[142] P.L. 112-96, Section 6209.
[143] P.L. 112-96, Section 6210.
[144] P.L. 112-96, Section 6001 (3).
[145] "Smart Grid" is the name given to the evolving electric power network as new information technology systems and capabilities are incorporated. See also CRS Report R41886, The Smart Grid and Cybersecurity—Regulatory Policy and Issues, by Richard J. Campbell.
[146] P.L. 112-96, Section 6206 (b) (1) (B).
[147] P.L. 112-96, Section 6206 (b) (1) (C).
[148] P.L. 112-96, Section 6206 (b) (3).
[149] P.L. 112-96, Section 6202 (a).
[150] P.L. 112-96, Section 6202 (b).
[151] P.L. 112-96, Section 6206 (c) (3).
[152] P.L. 112-96, Section 6206 (b) (3).
[153] P.L. 112-96, Section 6206, (c) (1).

[154] P.L. 112-96, Section 6206, (c) (2).
[155] P.L. 112-96, Section 6302 (e) (1).
[156] P.L. 112-96, Section 6302, (e) (2).
[157] P.L. 112-96, Section 6302, (e) (3) (B).
[158] P.L. 112-96, Section 6302 (e) (3) (C) (i).
[159] P.L. 112-96, Section 6302, (e) (3) (C) (iii).
[160] P.L. 112-96, Section 6302, (e) (3) (D) (i) (III).
[161] P.L. 112-96, Section 6503, "Section 158 "(a).
[162] P.L. 112-96, Section 6503, "Section 158 "(b).
[163] P.L. 112-96, Section 6503, "Section 158 "(c).
[164] P.L. 112-96, Section 6505.
[165] P.L. 112-96, Section 6504.
[166] P.L. 112-96, Section 6509.
[167] P.L. 112-96, Section 6507.
[168] P.L. 112-96, Section 6508.
[169] P.L. 112-96, Section 6506.
[170] P.L. 112-96, Section 6206 (b) (2) (C).
[171] FirstNet, Special Notice, "Operational Architecture Functional Descriptions," Figure 1 and Figure 2.
[172] FCC, Connecting America: The National Broadband Plan, http://www.broadband. gov/down load-plan/.
[173] P.L. 112-96, Section 6211.
[174] P.L. 112-95, Section 6206 (c) (5).
[175] P.L. 112-96 Section 6211.
[176] FCC, "Promoting Interoperability in the 700 MHZ Commercial Spectrum," Notice of Proposed Rulemaking, WT Docket No. 12-69, released March 21, 2012.
[177] FCC, "Report and Order and Order of Proposed Modification," WT Docket No. 12-69, released October 29, 2013.

In: The First Responder Network (FirstNet) ISBN: 978-1-63483-850-4
Editor: Margaret Saunders

Chapter 2

PUBLIC-SAFETY BROADBAND NETWORK: FIRSTNET SHOULD STRENGTHEN INTERNAL CONTROLS AND EVALUATE LESSONS LEARNED*

United States Government Accountability Office

WHY GAO DID THIS STUDY

For communications during emergencies, public safety officials rely on thousands of separate systems, which often lack interoperability, or the ability to communicate across agencies and jurisdictions. The 2012 act created FirstNet within the Department of Commerce to establish, for public safety use, a nationwide, interoperable, wireless broadband network, which will initially support data transmissions. The 2012 act established numerous responsibilities for FirstNet, provided $7 billion for network construction, and required FirstNet to be self-funding beyond this initial allocation. As part of the effort, FirstNet is working with five "early builder projects" that are building local and regional public-safety broadband networks.

GAO was asked to examine FirstNet's progress in establishing the network. GAO assessed (1) FirstNet's progress carrying out its responsibilities and establishing internal controls, (2) how much the network is estimated to

* This is an edited, reformatted and augmented version of the United States Government Accountability Office publication, GAO-15-407, dated April 2015.

cost and how FirstNet plans to become self- funding, and (3) what lessons can be learned from the early builder projects. GAO reviewed FirstNet documentation and public-safety network cost estimates, surveyed all state-designated FirstNet contacts, and interviewed FirstNet officials and public safety stakeholders selected for their telecommunications and public safety experience.

WHAT GAO RECOMMENDS

FirstNet should complete its risk assessment, develop standards of conduct, and develop an evaluation plan for early builder projects. FirstNet concurred with the recommendations.

WHAT GAO FOUND

The First Responder Network Authority (FirstNet) has made progress carrying out its responsibilities established in the Middle Class Tax Relief and Job Creation Act of 2012 (the 2012 act) but lacks certain elements of effective internal controls. FirstNet is charged with the complex and challenging task of establishing a new, nationwide, wireless broadband network for public safety entities, in consultation with federal, state, local, and tribal stakeholders. The network will initially support interoperable data communications, and later integrate mission-critical voice capabilities as public safety standards for voice communications are developed. FirstNet has made progress establishing an organizational structure, planning for the network, and consulting with stakeholders. FirstNet has also begun establishing policies and practices consistent with federal internal control standards. Officials told GAO that they plan to continue to do so. However, FirstNet has not fully assessed its risks or established standards of conduct—which is an important form of ethical guidance for its personnel. Given that FirstNet faces numerous risks to achieve its complex objectives, fully assessing risks could help FirstNet achieve its objectives and maximize use of its resources. Developing standards of conduct could also help FirstNet address any performance issues in a timely manner.

A nationwide public-safety broadband network has been estimated by various entities to cost billions of dollars, and FirstNet faces difficult decisions determining how to fund the network's construction and ongoing operations.

These estimates indicate the cost to construct and operate such a network could be from $12 to $47 billion over the first 10 years. The actual cost of FirstNet's network will be influenced by FirstNet's (1) business model, especially the extent of commercial partnerships; (2) use of existing infrastructure; (3) efforts to ensure network reliability; and (4) network coverage. For example, the cost of the network may be higher if FirstNet does not utilize partnerships and some existing infrastructure. To become self-funding, FirstNet is authorized to generate revenue through user fees and commercial partnerships. However, FirstNet faces difficult decisions in determining how to best utilize these revenue sources. For instance, widespread network coverage can attract more users and revenue, but is expensive to construct and maintain, especially in rural areas.

FirstNet has taken steps to collect and evaluate information and lessons from the five "early builder projects" that are developing local and regional public-safety networks, but could do more to ensure that the lessons are properly evaluated. For example, FirstNet has asked the projects to report on the experiences of their networks' users and has assigned contractors to collect and log lessons. However, FirstNet does not have a plan that clearly articulates how it will evaluate those experiences and lessons. Although FirstNet told GAO that it remains in close contact with early builder projects, GAO has previously found that a well-developed evaluation plan for projects like these can help ensure that agencies obtain the information necessary to make effective program and policy decisions. Given that the early builder projects are doing on a local and regional level what FirstNet must eventually do nationally, an evaluation plan can play a key role in FirstNet's strategic planning and program management, providing feedback on both program design and execution and ensuring FirstNet has not missed opportunities to incorporate lessons the projects have identified.

ABBREVIATIONS

2012 act	Middle Class Tax Relief and Job Creation Act of 2012
APA	Administrative Procedure Act
BTOP	Broadband Technology Opportunities Program
DHS	Department of Homeland Security
ECPC	Emergency Communications Preparedness Center
FAR	Federal Acquisition Regulation
FCC	Federal Communications Commission

FEMA	Federal Emergency Management Agency
FirstNet	First Responder Network Authority
LMR	land mobile radio
LTE	Long Term Evolution
NPSTC	National Public Safety Telecommunications Council
MHz	megahertz
NIST	National Institute of Standards and Technology
NOI	Notice of Inquiry
NTIA	National Telecommunications and Information Administration
OIG	Office of Inspector General
PSAC	Public Safety Advisory Committee
PSCR	Public Safety Communications Research
RAN	radio access network RFIRequest for Information
RFP	Request for Proposals
SLIGP	State and Local Implementation Grant Program
SMLA	Spectrum Manager Lease Agreement
SPOC	Single Point of Contact

* * *

April 28, 2015

The Honorable John Thune
Chairman
Committee on Commerce, Science and Transportation
United States Senate

Dear Mr. Chairman:

Communication systems are essential for public safety officials—especially first responders such as police, firefighters, and paramedics— to gather and share information during emergencies. First responders rely on thousands of separate, incompatible, and often proprietary land-mobile radio (LMR) systems for their mission-critical voice communications. Oftentimes these LMR systems lack "interoperability"—the capabilities that allow first responders to communicate with their counterparts in other agencies and jurisdictions with differing systems—which has been a long- standing concern. For example, during the terrorist attacks of September 11, 2001, and also during Hurricane Katrina in 2005, the lack of interoperable public-safety communications hampered rescue efforts and the overall effectiveness of public safety operations.

The Middle Class Tax Relief and Job Creation Act of 2012 provides resources, including both spectrum and billions of dollars, for the establishment of a nationwide, interoperable wireless broadband network specifically for first responders.[1] In particular, the 2012 act created the First Responder Network Authority (FirstNet) as an independent authority within the Department of Commerce's National Telecommunications and Information Administration (NTIA) to establish a nationwide public-safety broadband network,[2] allocated billions for its construction, and set aside radio frequency spectrum on which the network can operate.[3] The network is expected to support important data transmission (such as the vital signs of critically injured people and security-camera video feeds) and foster greater interoperability among public safety entities. Unlike current LMR systems, the devices operating on the public-safety broadband network are expected to be interoperable among first responders using the network, since they are using the same radio frequency band nationwide and will be required to be built to the same open, non-proprietary, commercially available standards.[4] The network will initially support data transmissions and non-mission critical voice, with mission-critical voice communications expected to be integrated in the coming years.

In developing the public-safety broadband network, FirstNet is faced with a complex and challenging mission. We previously reported on the challenges to implementing a public-safety broadband network, including ensuring the network's reliability and security and obtaining adequate funds to build and maintain it.[5] To inform its work, FirstNet is required to consult with numerous federal, state, local, and tribal jurisdictions.[6] FirstNet is also working with five "early builder projects" that received federal funding to deploy local and regional public-safety broadband networks similar to what FirstNet is required to establish on a national scale. FirstNet also has to develop a business plan that supports the upfront and ongoing costs of the public-safety broadband network.

You asked us to examine FirstNet's progress in establishing the nationwide public-safety broadband network. This report assesses (1) the extent to which FirstNet is carrying out its responsibilities and establishing internal controls for developing the public safety network, (2) how much the public safety network is estimated to cost to construct and operate and how

FirstNet plans to become a self-funding entity, and (3) what lessons can be learned from local and regional public-safety network early builder projects.

To address these objectives, we reviewed FirstNet's documentation, such as Requests for Information (RFI), annual reports to Congress, board- meeting materials and resolutions, and presentations to stakeholders. We compared FirstNet's efforts and progress to carry out its responsibilities with requirements established in the Middle Class Tax Relief and Job Creation Act of 2012[7] and compared FirstNet's efforts to establish internal controls with criteria established in the federal *Standards for Internal Control.*[8] We reviewed cost estimates for a nationwide public-safety broadband network from a variety of entities, including the Congressional Budget Office, the Federal Communications Commission (FCC), and academics.[9] We also reviewed FirstNet's cost estimate and conducted interviews with FirstNet officials to learn more about how the estimate was prepared, the assumptions underlying it, and the documentation supporting it. We assessed FirstNet's cost estimate against the criteria established in our *Cost Guide.*[10] We also interviewed early builder project officials from—and involved in—the five current projects (Los Angeles, CA; Adams County, CO; New Jersey; New Mexico; and Harris County, TX), three projects that were canceled (Charlotte, NC; Mississippi; and San Francisco, CA), and state and local public-safety entities in the project jurisdictions. We reviewed the Spectrum Manager Lease Agreements (SMLA) that each of the five current projects established with FirstNet, and documentation related to how FirstNet plans to collect lessons learned from the projects. We assessed FirstNet's plans to evaluate and utilize lessons from the projects against key features of a well-developed evaluation plan for pilot projects identified by our previous reports.[11]

To obtain stakeholder views, we surveyed all 50 states, the District of Columbia, and 5 U.S. territories. We administered the survey from October 2014 through November 2014 and received 55 responses, for a 98 percent response rate.[12] We interviewed FirstNet and NTIA officials and a variety of other stakeholders, such as state and local public-safety entities, commercial wireless carriers, subject matter experts, public safety associations, and federal agencies including FCC and the Department of Homeland Security (DHS). We also spoke with government officials in Sweden responsible for establishing a public- safety communications network in their country. We selected stakeholders by considering their involvement in the early builder project jurisdictions, experience with operating and using wireless communications systems and public-safety communications systems and devices in particular, familiarity with FirstNet and its mission, and—to obtain a cross-section of public safety disciplines—their public safety role.[13] More details about our scope and methodology can be found in appendix I and a copy of our survey in appendix II.

We conducted this performance audit from April 2014 to April 2015 in accordance with generally accepted government auditing standards. Those standards require that we plan and perform the audit to obtain sufficient, appropriate evidence to provide a reasonable basis for our findings and conclusions based on our audit objectives. We believe that the evidence obtained provides a reasonable basis for our findings and conclusions based on our audit objectives.

BACKGROUND

The Middle Class Tax Relief and Job Creation Act of 2012 (2012 act) established numerous responsibilities for FirstNet, most of which relate directly to developing the nationwide public-safety broadband network (hereafter, public safety network). It is intended that this network will be a new, nationwide, broadband telecommunications network. Public safety users, and potentially other "secondary" users,[14] may be assessed fees to use the network, much as they may currently pay for the use of commercial wireless networks. In establishing this network, FirstNet must

- issue open, transparent, and competitive Requests for Proposals (RFP) to private sector entities for the purpose of building, operating, and maintaining the public safety network;
- develop RFPs that include appropriate timetables for construction, and network coverage areas and service levels, among other things;
- enter into agreements to use, to the maximum extent economically desirable, existing commercial, federal, state, local, and tribal infrastructure;
- promote competition in the public-safety equipment marketplace by requiring that equipment for the public safety network be built to open, non-proprietary standards;
- promote integration of the public safety network with public-safety answering points;
- address special considerations for areas with unique homeland or national security needs;

- require deployment phases that include substantial rural coverage milestones; and
- develop the technical and operational requirements for the public safety network, as well as the practices and procedures for managing and operating it.

In establishing the infrastructure for the public safety network, the 2012 act requires FirstNet to include the following network components, as shown in figure 1:[15]

- core network of data centers and other elements, all based on commercial standards;
- connectivity between the radio access network (RAN) and the public Internet or the Public Switched Telephone Network, or both; and
- network cell-site equipment, antennas, and "backhaul" equipment, based on commercial standards, to support wireless devices operating on frequencies designated for public safety broadband.[16]

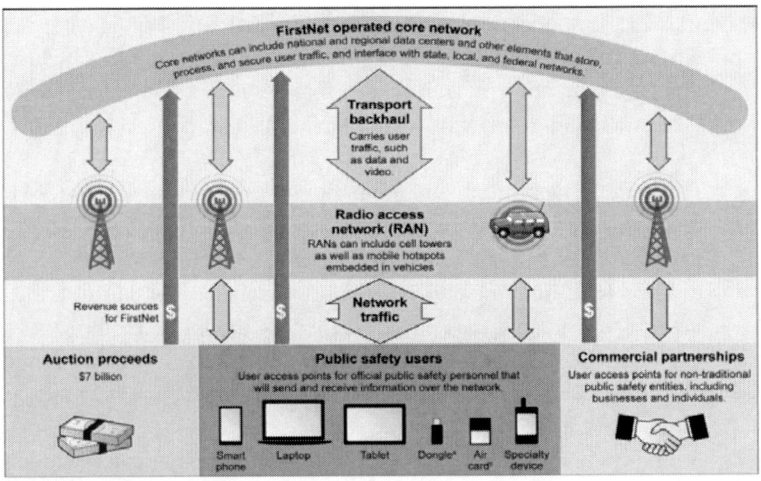

Source GAO | GAO-15-407

[a] Generally, "dongles" are small devices that plug into computers and serve as an adapter or as a security measure to enable the use of certain software.

[b] Generally, "air cards" are wireless adapters for sending and receiving data in a cellular network.

Figure 1. Key Elements of First Responder Network Authority's (FirstNet) Public Safety Network.

In developing the public safety network, FirstNet must work with a variety of stakeholders. The 2012 act required FirstNet to be headed by a 15- member board with 3 permanent members (the Secretary of Homeland Security, the Attorney General, and the Director of the Office of Management and Budget) and 12 individuals appointed by the Secretary of Commerce. The appointed members are required to have public safety experience or technical, network, or financial expertise.[17] The 2012 act also required FirstNet to establish a standing public-safety advisory committee to assist it in carrying out its responsibilities and consult with federal, regional, state, local, and tribal jurisdictions on developing the network.[18] For state, local, and tribal planning consultations, FirstNet is required to work with the state Single Points of Contact (SPOC) who have been designated by each state, territory, and the District of Columbia (hereafter, states).[19]

The 2012 act requires FirstNet to notify the states when it has completed its RFP process for building, operating, and maintaining the public safety network.[20] Once a state receives the details of FirstNet's plans, it has 90 days either to agree to allow FirstNet to construct a RAN in that state or notify FirstNet, NTIA, and FCC of its intent to deploy its own RAN. A state that "opts out" of FirstNet's plan to build that state's RAN has an additional 180 days from that notification to develop and complete RFPs for the construction, maintenance, and operation of the RAN within the state; the state must send FCC an alternative plan for constructing, operating, and maintaining its RAN. The plan must demonstrate that the state's proposed RAN would comply with certain minimum technical requirements and be interoperable with FirstNet's network. FCC shall either approve or disapprove the plan. In addition, a state that opts out is required to apply to NTIA for an agreement to use FirstNet's spectrum capacity.

Various federal agencies will provide assistance and support to FirstNet. For example,

- The National Institute of Standards and Technology (NIST) within the Department of Commerce, in consultation with FCC, DHS, and the Department of Justice's National Institute of Justice, is required to conduct research and assist with the development of standards, technologies, and applications to advance wireless public-safety communications.[21]
- The Public Safety Communications Research (PSCR) program, a joint NTIA and NIST effort, performs research on behalf of FirstNet to advance public-safety communications interoperability.[22]

- DHS, through both the Office of Emergency Communications and the Office for Interoperability and Compatibility, supports the establishment of the public safety network and collaborates with public safety and government officials at the federal, state, local, and tribal levels to help ensure the network meets the needs and technical requirements of users in the public safety community.

The 2012 act also required FCC, the entity responsible for managing and licensing commercial and non-federal spectrum use—including spectrum allocated to public safety—to take certain steps to support FirstNet. It also authorized FCC to provide FirstNet with technical assistance and to take any action necessary to assist FirstNet in effectuating its statutory duties and responsibilities. Radio frequency spectrum is an essential resource for wireless communications, including the planned public-safety network. The energy in electronic telecommunications transmissions converts airwaves into signals to deliver voice, text, and images. These signal frequencies are allocated for specific purposes, such as television broadcasting or Wi-Fi, and assigned to specific users through licenses.

Allocating sufficient spectrum for wireless emergency communications has long been a concern for Congress. The 2012 act required FCC to reallocate the "D Block," a previously commercial spectrum block located in the upper 700 megahertz (MHz) band, to public safety[23] and to grant a license to FirstNet for the use of both the existing public-safety broadband spectrum in the upper 700 MHz band and the D Block.[24] FirstNet now has a license to operate the nationwide public-safety broadband network on spectrum in the upper 700 MHz band, specifically 758-769 MHz and 788-799 MHz (see fig. 2 below). In October 2013, FCC adopted consolidated technical service rules governing the 700 MHz band of spectrum licensed to FirstNet and was prepared to accept and process applications for equipment certification in that spectrum band consistent with the newly consolidated rules.[25] FCC has conducted specified spectrum auctions, as required by the 2012 act, so that auction proceeds could be used to fund FirstNet.[26] The 2012 act provides $7 billion from the spectrum auction proceeds to FirstNet for "buildout" of the public safety network, reduced by the amount needed to establish FirstNet.[27] The 2012 act requires FirstNet to be self-funding beyond this initial $7 billion.[28]

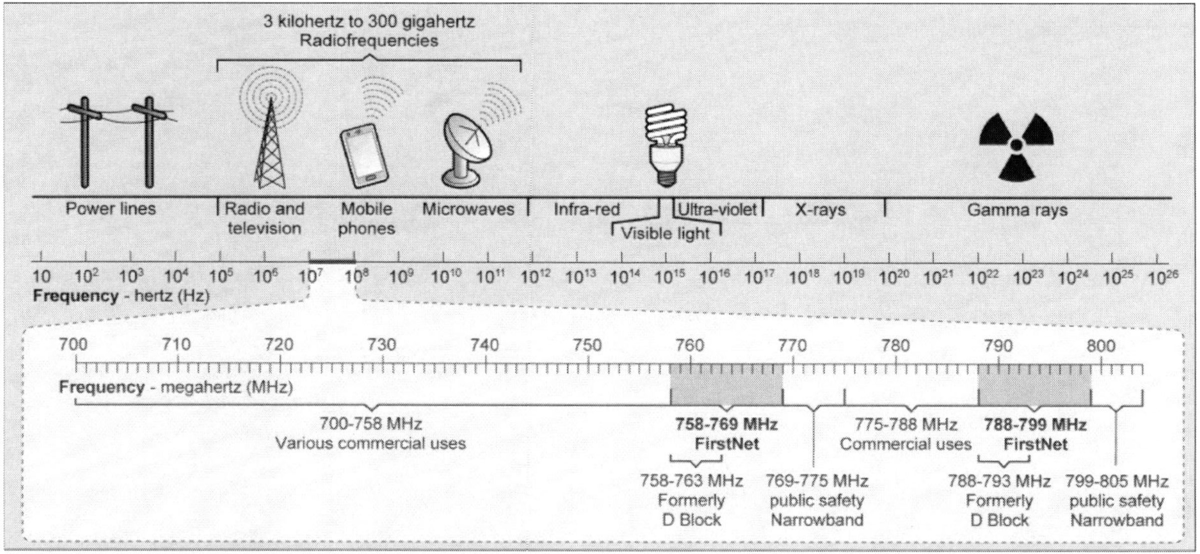

Source: Federal Communication Commission and GAO. | GAO-15-407

Figure 2. First Responder Network Authority's (FirstNet) Spectrum.

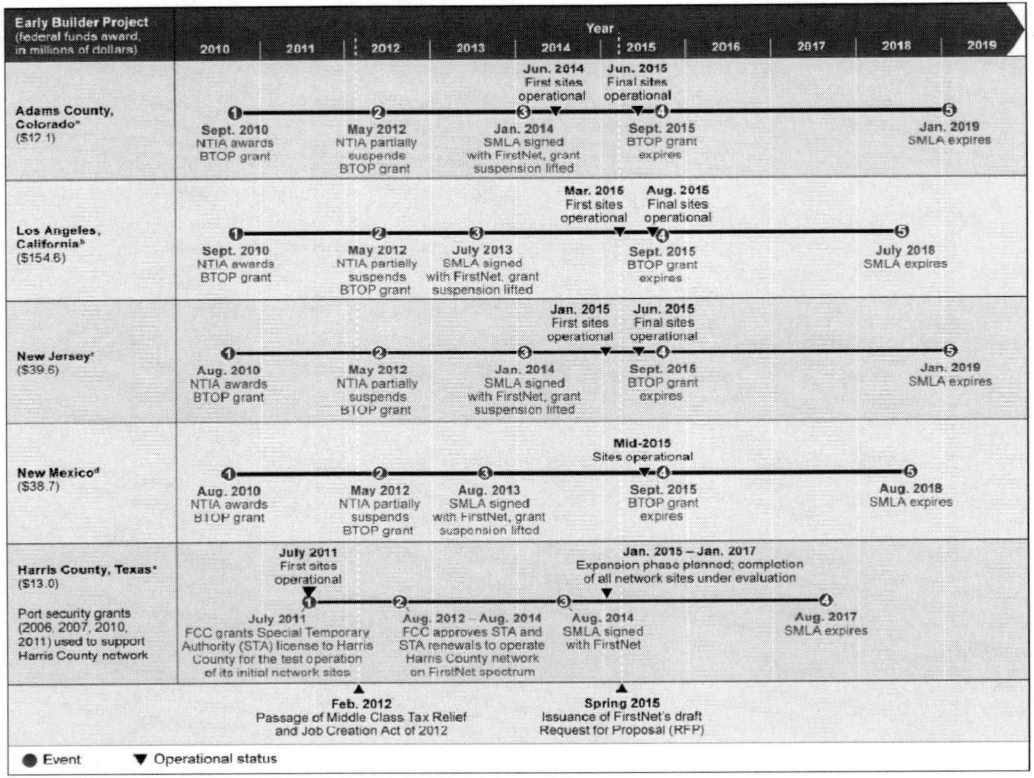

Source: GAO based on information from Spectrum Manager Lease Agreements (SMLAs), Early Builder Projects, National Telecommunication and information Administration (NTIA), Broadband Technology Opportunities Program (BTOP)

documentation, Federal Communication Commission (FCC) documentation, and the First Responder Network Authority (FirstNet), First and final sites operational information provides by project official | GAO-15-407

[a] FirstNet entered into an SMLA with the Adams County Communications Center, Inc., which plans to provide broadband network coverage for Adams County, Colorado.

[b] FirstNet entered into an SMLA with the Los Angeles Regional Interoperable Communications System Authority, which plans to provide broadband network coverage to over 4,000 square miles of geographic boundaries around Los Angeles, California.

[c] FirstNet entered into an SMLA with the State of New Jersey by and through the Office of Information Technology. While the Office of Information Technology will continue to be the primary recipient of the BTOP grant, project activities have been transitioned to the New Jersey Office of Homeland Security and Preparedness, which will implement deployable public-safety broadband networks in three service regions including Atlantic City, Camden, and the "Route 21 Corridor" or state highway in north central New Jersey.

[d] FirstNet entered into an SMLA with the State of New Mexico, which plans to focus its public-safety broadband network on the southwest border area.

[e] FirstNet entered into an SMLA with the State of Texas, which plans to provide broadband network coverage for Harris County, Texas.

Figure 3. Early Builder Project Timelines, as of January 2015.

Efforts to establish local and regional public-safety networks are also ongoing, and predate the 2012 act. In 2009, public safety entities began requesting waivers from FCC's rules to allow early deployment of interoperable public-safety wireless broadband networks in the upper 700 MHz spectrum band authorized for public safety use. Through 2011, FCC granted waivers to 22 jurisdictions for early deployment of such networks.[29] However, FCC recognized that the 2012 act "fundamentally altered the regulatory landscape for the 700 MHz band" and sought comment on the disposition of waiver jurisdiction deployments.[30] In May 2012, NTIA partially suspended seven grant projects for the waiver jurisdictions that received funding from the Broadband Technology Opportunities Program (BTOP), a federal grant program to promote the expansion of broadband infrastructure.[31] NTIA suspended the projects in part to ensure the projects supported the development of FirstNet's public safety network. In July 2012, FCC decided to hold all waiver authorizations ineffective as of September 2, 2012, and said it would allow such jurisdictions to continue to deploy public-safety broadband services in the existing public-safety broadband spectrum (later extended to include the D Block) under certain limited circumstances consistent with FirstNet's future use of the spectrum.[32] FCC granted FirstNet the 700 MHz public-safety broadband-spectrum license in November 2012,[33] and in February 2013, FirstNet announced it would begin negotiations with the original waiver jurisdictions on SMLAs. With FirstNet in control of the 700 MHz public-safety broadband-spectrum license pursuant to its FCC license, the jurisdictions had to secure an SMLA with FirstNet to lift their partial funding suspension and resume work. By August 2014, FirstNet secured SMLAs with five original waiver jurisdictions; in this report, we refer to these jurisdictions as early builder projects. Figure 3 shows timelines for the early builder projects and the amount of federal funding they received to deploy their networks. As part of their SMLAs with FirstNet, the early builder projects agreed to report to FirstNet on their use of the spectrum, their progress, and on key-learning conditions, among other things. FirstNet has not yet determined if or how the early builder project networks will be incorporated into its nationwide network.[34]

Three other original waiver jurisdictions were awarded BTOP funds to deploy local and regional public-safety broadband networks, including the State of Mississippi,[35] the San Francisco Bay Area in California,[36] and the City of Charlotte in North Carolina.[37] However, for various reasons, these jurisdictions were unable to reach SMLAs with FirstNet and the projects were canceled.

Even with the establishment of the public safety network, first responders will continue to rely on their current LMR systems for mission-critical voice communications. We previously reported that a major limitation of a public-safety broadband network is that it will not provide first responders with "mission-critical" voice capabilities—that is, voice capabilities that meet a high standard for reliability, redundancy, capacity, and flexibility necessary during emergencies—for several years.[38] Long Term Evolution (LTE), the technical standard for the public-safety broadband network, is a wireless broadband standard that is not currently designed to support mission-critical voice communications.[39] Commercial wireless providers are currently providing voice over LTE capabilities, but these capabilities do not currently meet public safety's mission-critical voice requirements because key elements needed for mission-critical voice—such as group calls—are not part of the LTE standard. Therefore, public safety agencies will continue to rely on their LMR systems for mission-critical voice for the foreseeable future, and the public safety network will supplement, rather than replace, current LMR systems.

FirstNet Is Making Progress Meeting Responsibilities but Lacks Certain Elements of Effective Internal Controls

FirstNet Is Making Progress Carrying Out Statutory Responsibilities

FirstNet has made progress carrying out its statutory responsibilities in three areas—(1) establishing its organizational structure, (2) planning the public safety network, and (3) consulting with stakeholders—but could face challenges in each of these areas. Figure 4 provides a timeline of select events in FirstNet's progress meeting its statutory responsibilities since the 2012 act's passage.

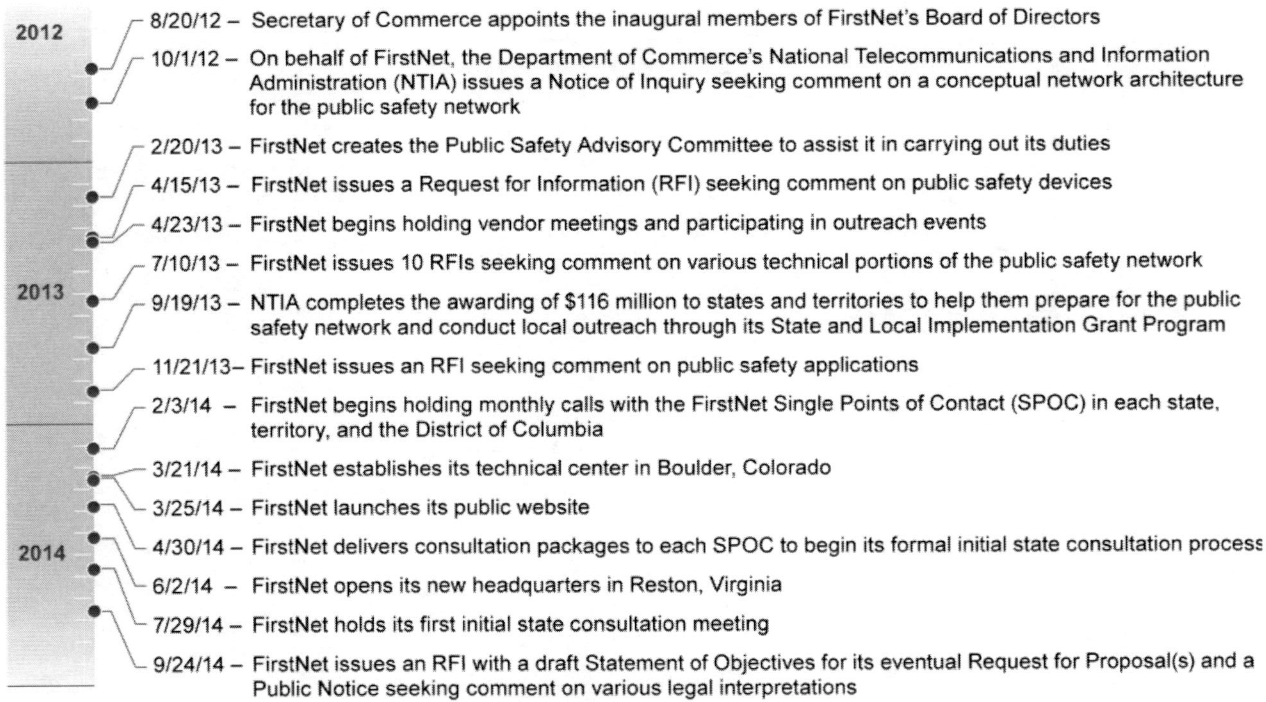

Source: GAO based on FirstNet and NTIA information | GAO-15-407

Figure 4. Select Events in the First Responder Network Authority's (FirstNet) Efforts since Establishment in February 2012.

Source: GAO based on FirstNet information | GAO-15-407

[a] This position is a planned future position. New officer positions may be created at the discretion of the Board of Directors.

Figure 5. First Responder Network Authority (FirstNet) Organizational Structure, as of February 2015.

Establishing Its Organizational Structure

As a newly created entity within the federal government, FirstNet has taken a number of steps to establish its organizational structure and hire staff. As required by the 2012 act, the Secretary of Commerce appointed FirstNet's inaugural board members in August 2012.[40] FirstNet's Board established Governance and Personnel, Finance, Technology, and Outreach Committees to review, approve, and oversee FirstNet's activities. As required by the 2012 act, FirstNet's Board also established the Public Safety Advisory Committee (PSAC) in February 2013—one year after the 2012 act's passage—and adopted the PSAC's charter in June 2014.[41] The PSAC's membership represents a broad cross section of public safety disciplines and state, local, and tribal governments. In addition to the board and the PSAC, FirstNet has established organizational units and hired key personnel to lead and perform its work. In April 2013—over a year after the 2012 act's passage—the FirstNet Board selected an Executive Director to lead its day-to-day operations.[42] Since then, FirstNet has hired, and continues to hire, other senior management personnel to lead its organizational units (such as a Chief Counsel and Chief Administrative, Financial, and Information Officers), and Directors and organizational chiefs to further lead and perform its work. FirstNet has also hired, and continues to hire, general staff. As of February 2015, FirstNet had over 120 employees, including full-time equivalent federal employees, contractors, and personnel on detail from other agencies. FirstNet confirmed in February 2015 that it may hire up to 42 additional full-time equivalent federal employees in fiscal year 2015 and that it will evaluate and adjust needed staffing levels on an ongoing basis. See figure 5 for an overview of FirstNet's organizational structure. Additionally, in June 2014, FirstNet opened its "corporate" headquarters in Reston, Virginia, and, in March 2014, a technical center to serve as its technical, engineering, and network design headquarters in Boulder, Colorado.

Stakeholders we spoke with and surveyed expressed concern that organizational issues have slowed FirstNet's progress and could continue to do so. In particular, in response to our survey, numerous SPOCs noted either that FirstNet's placement within NTIA could create "bureaucratic" obstacles or that FirstNet should be more independent from NTIA. One survey respondent and another subject matter expert we interviewed also noted that this placement creates conflicting expectations—that is, stakeholders expect FirstNet to behave like both a commercial wireless carrier and a government entity, and these expectations can sometimes be in conflict. However, FirstNet officials told us that while FirstNet has leveraged its relationship with NTIA in administrative and legal matters, it exercises strong independence in decisions that are directly program- related.

Numerous stakeholders we surveyed and interviewed were also concerned about the pace of FirstNet's hiring, noting that the federal hiring process is too slow, has not allowed FirstNet to hire staff quickly enough, and has delayed FirstNet's progress. For example, FirstNet hired its management team for state plans, consultation, and outreach in late 2013 to early 2014, then hired State and Local, Tribal, and Federal Outreach Leads in June and August 2014, almost 2 years after FirstNet's board members were appointed. Additionally, FirstNet is still in the process of hiring staff for key positions. For example, as of February 2015 FirstNet was re-filling the Chief User Advocacy Officer and Director of Communications positions, was planning for the hiring of a Chief Procurement Officer, and was in the process of hiring staff to lead regional consultation teams that it plans to establish, among other positions.[43] As of February 2015, it was also still hiring key technical positions—including Director of Devices, Director of Standards, and Director of Core Network—and re-filling the Chief Technology Officer position. According to FirstNet officials, FirstNet faces challenges hiring as quickly as it would like, in part due to government hiring procedures, but is seeking direct hire authority from the Office of Personnel Management and is exploring other authorities it could use to expedite hiring.[44]

Planning the Public Safety Network

To plan the public safety network and help ensure that its approach is open and transparent and meets the 2012 act's requirements and that interested parties have a formal way to comment on FirstNet's strategy and decisions, FirstNet intends to follow the Federal Acquisition Regulation (FAR) process for its comprehensive network-services procurement.[45] This process will culminate in one or multiple RFPs for "network solution(s)"—that is, proposals for the building, deployment, operation, and maintenance of the public safety network. To help draft the RFP(s), FirstNet has sought comments through a Notice of Inquiry (NOI), RFIs, and Public Notices. Specifically, in October 2012, NTIA, on behalf of FirstNet, issued an NOI to seek input on the network's potential architecture.[46] From April to November 2013, FirstNet issued 12 detailed RFIs on specific technical aspects of the network and on devices and applications for public safety. NTIA and FirstNet received over 400 comments to the NOI and RFIs, and FirstNet has used these as a source of market research in assessing industry capabilities and developing the technical design of the network. Building off these efforts, in September 2014 FirstNet issued an RFI that sought further comment on a number of issues, such as network coverage, pricing, deployment strategies, security, prioritization among network users, and customer service, among other things. According to this RFI, FirstNet's current approach is to follow a performance-based procurement strategy, whereby FirstNet does not dictate the specific network solution that bidders responding to the RFP(s) must provide, but, rather, outlines objectives and encourages bidders to develop proposals that will meet those objectives.[47]

Additionally, although the 2012 act exempts FirstNet from portions of the Administrative Procedure Act (APA), FirstNet has chosen to follow an APA-like process in order to provide more opportunities for interested parties to comment on its interpretations of the 2012 act's requirements.[48]

Therefore, in September 2014, FirstNet also issued a Public Notice seeking comment on a number of its preliminary interpretations, such as how to define its rural coverage milestones and eligible network users.[49]

FirstNet received 185 responses to the September 2014 RFI and Public Notice from a broad range of respondents, such as states, public safety entities, private companies, and associations. FirstNet issued a second Public Notice in March 2015 and expects to issue a draft RFP in spring 2015.

In addition to its efforts seeking public comment, FirstNet has also received technical input from a variety of stakeholders, such as FCC, the PSAC, the National Public Safety Telecommunications Council (NPSTC), and the PSCR program.[50] As required by the 2012 act, the FCC's Technical Advisory Board for First Responder Interoperability issued minimum technical requirements for the public safety network in May 2012.[51] The report provided recommendations on LTE standards; network user equipment, device management, and evolution; and quality of service, among other things. FirstNet has also asked the PSAC to provide recommendations on various topics, including a framework for establishing the priority of public safety entities on the network.[52] In May 2014, NPSTC provided FirstNet with guidance on what makes communication systems "public-safety grade."[53] Additionally, FirstNet has provided the PSCR—which is based in Boulder, Colorado, where FirstNet's technical center is also located—with funding to research interoperability standards, test and evaluate potential network features, and model and simulate network data traffic.

Notwithstanding this progress, stakeholders maintained that developing a nationwide public-safety network will pose challenges. Numerous stakeholders we interviewed—such as SPOCs; federal, state, and local public-safety entities; public safety associations; commercial wireless carriers; and individual experts—cited upcoming difficulties. For example, they noted that deciding the level of network coverage and security, working out agreements for use of existing infrastructure, resolving questions about user priority, and navigating state regulations will be difficult to address. In response to our survey, the SPOCs most frequently responded that they were "neither satisfied nor dissatisfied" with FirstNet's progress on various responsibilities related to developing the network.[54] SPOCs were most satisfied with FirstNet's progress carrying out a transparent RFI process and most dissatisfied with FirstNet's progress developing the technical and operational requirements of the network, and the practices, procedures, and standards for managing and operating the network. Still, even in these instances, SPOCs' level of satisfaction or dissatisfaction was mostly "moderate."[55] While many stakeholders we surveyed and interviewed noted that FirstNet's progress has been too slow, some also noted that they were satisfied with FirstNet's progress given the complex nature of FirstNet's tasks and that it is a government entity subject to federal rules and regulations. Some also said that FirstNet's progress has improved recently, especially as FirstNet has hired more staff.

Consulting Stakeholders

FirstNet has initiated a process to consult with the public safety community in each state through the SPOC. FirstNet first worked to establish informal mechanisms for coordinating with the SPOCs. For example, FirstNet began holding regional workshops in May 2013, quarterly SPOC webinars in January 2014, and monthly calls with SPOCs in February 2014. FirstNet began its formal state consultation process by delivering an initial consultation package to each SPOC in April 2014; the package contained a checklist for the SPOCs to complete in preparation for an initial consultation meeting. FirstNet is using these meetings to gather information on each state's unique challenges, needs, and processes to inform its development of the public safety network and, in particular, state RAN plans. Initial state consultation meetings began in July 2014—when FirstNet conducted its first consultation with Maryland— and FirstNet expects these initial meetings to continue through 2015, with additional rounds to follow. As of April 16, 2015, FirstNet had conducted initial consultation meetings with 18 states, Puerto Rico, and the District of Columbia.

In addition to its consultation with SPOCs, FirstNet officials have conducted outreach to other stakeholders. For example, from October 2013 to February 2015, FirstNet officials visited 39 states and territories while participating in 187 events, such as state town halls and public safety, industry, and government (including federal, state, local, and tribal) conferences. To engage with tribal entities, FirstNet staff visited eight tribal nations in 2014, and sought the advice of the PSAC on tribal outreach, education, and inclusive consultation strategies.[56] To engage with federal entities, FirstNet has hired a director of federal outreach, designated DHS's Emergency Communications Preparedness Center (ECPC) as the primary body to FirstNet for federal consultation, and participated in meetings with ECPC and other agencies. To engage with vendors interested in doing business with FirstNet, FirstNet has held vendor meetings and appointed an industry liaison to coordinate vendor outreach. In addition to this targeted outreach, FirstNet also launched a public website in March 2014, where it regularly posts updates, presentations, board-meeting minutes, a list of upcoming speaking engagements, and other information. The 2012 act also created a State and Local Implementation Grant Program (SLIGP), administered by NTIA, to provide states with funds to plan for the public safety network and to consult with FirstNet.[57] Starting in July 2013, NTIA awarded $116 million in SLIGP grants.[58]

We believe FirstNet's consultation and outreach activities generally align with core principles for effective stakeholder participation that we have developed and used in previous reports.[59] For example, we found during the course of our review that FirstNet is using an open and clearly defined decision-making process, actively conducting outreach, involving stakeholders throughout the process, using formal and informal participation methods, and including all stakeholders.

The majority of stakeholders we surveyed were generally satisfied with the level of FirstNet's consultation and outreach, but others were dissatisfied and said that they would like more new information. In response to our survey, 54 percent of SPOCs said they were either "moderately" or "very" satisfied with FirstNet's overall level of consultation, coordination, and communication, while 22 percent said they were either "moderately" or "very" dissatisfied.[60] However, numerous stakeholders we surveyed and interviewed said that they would like more new and detailed information and that they would like FirstNet to focus more on certain aspects of the public safety network during outreach. For example, in response to our survey, SPOCs most frequently indicated that there should be a "large increase" in how much FirstNet focuses on various technical aspects of developing the network in its state outreach.[61] Some SPOCs also said that the lack of new information from FirstNet, such as details about the network's design, hampers their ability to conduct local outreach. However, in response to our survey many SPOCs also acknowledged that the level of new and detailed information exchanged will likely increase once they hold their initial state consultation meeting with FirstNet. Additionally, officials from one federal agency with public safety responsibilities said they would have liked to see more in-depth outreach to federal entities, given that federal agencies will have a large pool of potential network users. In January 2015, FirstNet formally initiated its federal consultation process. As part of this process, FirstNet will conduct meetings with federal entities in 2015 similar to the initial consultation meetings it is conducting with states.

FirstNet Has Not Assessed Risk or Established a Complete Control Environment

Internal controls are the plans, methods, policies, and procedures that an entity uses to fulfill its mission, strategic plan, goals, and objectives. An effective internal control system increases the likelihood that an entity will achieve its objectives. We assessed FirstNet's policies and practices against two components of an effective federal internal control system: risk assessment and control environment.[62] We chose to assess these two components because risk assessment provides the basis for developing appropriate risk responses and control activities and the control environment is the foundation for an internal control system. For those two components, we found that—although FirstNet has begun establishing policies and practices that are consistent with federal standards—FirstNet lacked certain elements that contribute to the proper implementation of effective internal control systems. While FirstNet has stated that it is relying on the Department of Commerce's and NTIA's internal controls where it has not developed its own, it is also important for FirstNet to implement its own controls, as the Commerce Office of Inspector General (OIG) noted as early as February 2014 in a memo on the management challenges facing FirstNet.

Risk Assessment

In an internal control system, according to federal internal control standards, management should assess risks facing the entity as it seeks to achieve its objectives. Specifically, entities should first clearly define their objectives then identify and analyze risks from both internal and external sources. Analyzing risks generally includes estimating the risk's significance, assessing the likelihood of its occurrence, and deciding how to respond to it. Risk assessments inform an entity's policies, planning, and priorities, and help entities develop responses to the risks they face, so that they can achieve their objectives. Control activities respond to these risks.

FirstNet has set objectives and taken some steps to assess risks. Specifically, FirstNet has set three key objectives:

1. Provide FirstNet services that are critical to public safety users and differentiate FirstNet services from commercial broadband services, such as through reliability, resiliency, coverage, functionality, interoperability, quality of service, priority access, pre-emption, and applications.
2. Reduce costs for public safety entities by leveraging the value of excess network capacity with partners.
3. Provide mechanisms for public safety entities (directly or indirectly through the states) to benefit from the economies of scale created by FirstNet in terms of purchasing, partnering, and information/data.

FirstNet has further delineated how it will accomplish these objectives in a "roadmap" that identifies additional long-term and short-term objectives and milestones.[63] FirstNet has established a Program Management Office to, according to FirstNet officials, help set internal timelines and monitor the completion of tasks needed to achieve these objectives and reach these milestones. Additionally, the Department of Commerce and FirstNet have performed some risk assessment activities. In February 2014, the Commerce OIG issued a memorandum outlining the top management challenges facing FirstNet. To support development of the roadmap, FirstNet created a "risk register" that identifies some risks related to its financial sustainability as well as possible counter-measures.[64]

However, FirstNet has not yet fully assessed risks it may face in accomplishing its objectives. FirstNet officials told us in November 2014 that they have not yet done so because they are in the process of defining risk factors and, again in December 2014, because they are in the process of conducting a legal compliance risk assessment of certain key risk areas. In December 2014, FirstNet officials also said that they intend to perform periodic risk assessments in various areas to manage and mitigate risks on an iterative basis.[65] However, as of February 2015, FirstNet has not yet completed these risk assessment activities. As a result, we were unable to evaluate the extent to which these activities align with the elements of risk assessment detailed in the federal internal control standards, and therefore, it remains unclear how effective FirstNet's efforts will be in helping it to identify and respond to obstacles to fulfilling its responsibilities.

As FirstNet completes these assessments, we believe that it is important that it incorporate all of the elements of risk assessment detailed in the federal internal control standards. Lacking complete risk assessments (that is, assessments that incorporate these elements), FirstNet's control activities may not be designed to respond to the appropriate risks. In previous work, we found that when an agency worked quickly to establish a new program, it resulted in the agency's hastily designing an internal control system that was not based on complete risk assessments and that the agency responded to risks in a reactive, rather than a proactive, manner. Thus, it was unclear whether the controls appropriately responded to risk or were the best use of the agency's resources.[66]

Additionally, we are concerned that the complexity of FirstNet's responsibilities and objectives, makeup of FirstNet's Board of Directors, and challenges that FirstNet will face attracting users to its network and becoming self-funding illustrate the multitude of potential risks FirstNet faces in achieving its objectives. For example, as we point out later in this report, various factors could hinder whether public safety entities adopt the public safety network—and thus how much user fee revenue FirstNet can collect—which could pose risks to FirstNet's ability to become self- funding. Given this, complete risk assessments could help FirstNet appropriately design its full internal control system and achieve its objectives while maximizing use of its available resources.

Control Environment

The control environment is the foundation for an internal control system and provides the basic structure that helps an entity achieve its objectives. To help set this environment, according to federal internal control standards, an entity should

- establish an organizational structure and delegate authority throughout the entity;
- establish appropriate human-capital practices for hiring, developing, evaluating, retaining, supervising, and disciplining personnel;
- demonstrate a commitment to competence, such as by establishing expectations of competence and holding personnel accountable by evaluating their performance;

- demonstrate a commitment to integrity and ethical values, such as by setting a positive "tone at the top," providing and evaluating adherence to ethical and behavioral guidance, and removing temptations for unethical behavior; and
- have an oversight body that oversees the entity's internal control system.

FirstNet has taken a number of steps to begin establishing an effective control environment. As described above, FirstNet has established an organizational structure with clearly designated responsibilities and has explored hiring options that would allow it to recruit individuals more quickly. According to FirstNet officials, to develop staff, FirstNet has also leveraged its relationship with the Department of Commerce by using the Department's training facilities as it works to create FirstNet-specific training. Per Department of Commerce policy, FirstNet's Senior Executive Service employees are subject to applicable competency and evaluation plans and other employees are evaluated using a performance appraisal process. Additionally, FirstNet has taken steps to identify and manage potential conflicts of interest. For example, FirstNet has held ethics briefings, distributed ethics documents, held ethics counseling and training, and instituted a Board Member Vendor Interaction Policy to establish processes for board members interacting with vendors with a potential interest in FirstNet's procurement efforts. FirstNet has also established and disseminated a variety of guidance documents, such as policies on employee timekeeping, expenses, travel, information technology rules of behavior, and telework. Finally, FirstNet's Board Committees and FirstNet senior management's Compliance Committee oversee FirstNet's activities and the Commerce OIG and others perform additional oversight.[67]

However, FirstNet has not yet finished establishing its control environment. While FirstNet has a variety of separate guidelines and policies, it does not have a uniform and cohesive standards of conduct policy. Specifically, although FirstNet officials told us that they intend to develop a code/standards of conduct policy, which is an important form of ethical and behavioral guidance for personnel, they have not yet developed this item as of February 2015. According to FirstNet officials, FirstNet has not yet done so because, as a "start-up" entity, building up the organization while making progress meeting statutory responsibilities is a balancing act affected by FirstNet's priorities and resources.

Nonetheless, absent standards of conduct, we are concerned that FirstNet may not be able to address deviations in its personnel's conduct and performance, and take corrective actions in a timely manner. Indeed, FirstNet itself established a special committee in May 2013 to review ethical concerns raised by one of its board members. Similarly, in a December 2014 report, the Commerce OIG identified concerns with FirstNet's financial disclosure reporting and contracting practices, among other things.[68] The report highlighted that the FirstNet Board, out of necessity, includes members with significant ties to the telecommunications industry that make strategic decisions regarding FirstNet's operations and, thus, are at increased risk of encountering conflicts of interests. Although FirstNet has taken corrective actions since the Commerce OIG's investigation, we believe that establishing and evaluating adherence to standards of conduct may help FirstNet ensure that all its personnel are held accountable for their actions. By establishing this item, FirstNet could also foster stakeholder trust in its ability to meet its statutory responsibilities and be a good steward of public funds.

FirstNet Faces Difficult Decisions in Determining How to Pay for a Nationwide Public-Safety Network Estimated to Cost Billions

Cost of a Public Safety Network Estimated to Be at least $12 Billion over First 10 Years

Various entities have estimated the cost to construct and operate a nationwide network for public safety from a low of $12 billion to a high of between $34 and $47 billion, over the first 10 years. As shown in table 1, a variety of entities have developed cost estimates for a public-safety broadband network, although they have used different assumptions about the network's scope. Key assumptions influencing these estimates include whether the network is constructed, operated, or financed in partnership with commercial entities, and the number of sites needed to provide the network's coverage. For instance, FCC's 2010 estimate assumes costs would be decreased through a high level of cooperation with commercial carriers. These estimates also vary, for instance, on how much they expect ongoing maintenance and operation to cost. However, some differences among these estimates are difficult to identify since some of the estimates do not explicitly state all their assumptions.

Table 1. Selected Cost Estimates for Constructing a Public-Safety Broadband Network

Source	Year of estimate[a]	Commercial partnership	Coverage (percent of population)	Sites	Cost per site (thousands)	Up-Front deployment costs (billions)[b]	Total costs, first 10 years(billions)[c]
Cyren Call Communications Corporation	2007	Yes	99	37,000	No estimate	$18[d]	No estimate
Eisenach	2007	Yes	99	33,700	$600,000	No estimate	$20
Federal Communications Commission	2010	Yes	99	44,800	$140,625[e]	$7	$12-16
		No	99	44,800	$350,446[e]	$16	$34-47
Hallahan and Peha	2010	Yes	99	19,400	$500,000	$10	$18
		No	99	22,200	$500,000	$11	$20
Congressional Budget Office	2011	Yes	95	45,000	No estimate	No estimate	$12

Sources: Sachs, Elizabeth, on behalf of Cyren Call Communications, *In the Matter of Public Safety Network in the 700 MHz Broadband,* Ex Parte Presentation to Federal Communications Commission (June 3, 2007); Eisenach, Jeffrey, *Due Diligence: Risk Factors in the Frontline Proposal (*June 28, 2007); Federal Communications Commission (FCC), *A Broadband Network Cost Model: A Basis for Public Funding Essential to Bringing Nationwide Interoperable Communications to America's First Responders*, OBI Technical Paper No. 2 (May 2010); Hallahan, Ryan, and John M. Peha, *Quantifying the Costs of a Nationwide Public Safety Wireless Network*, Telecommunications Policy, 34 (2010); Congressional Budget Office, *Cost Estimate: S. 911 Public Safety Spectrum and Wireless Innovation Act* (July 2011). | GAO-15-407

[a] The figures are presented here as they were reported at the time of publication; that is, we did not adjust these figures for inflation.

[b] Estimates vary in scope, with some estimating the total cost and some only considering costs associated with the installation and operation of cell sites and not the costs of the backbone network components, or the costs of network planning and administration.

[c] The total costs include both the up-front deployment costs plus ongoing costs, such as maintenance and operations, over the first 10 years.

[d] This estimate is described as including "cumulative capital expenditures." It is not clear whether this only includes up-front deployments costs or also some (or all) maintenance and operations over the first 10 years.

[e] This is an average cost across all proposed sites. FCC estimated different costs for sites in urban, suburban, and rural areas.

The actual costs per site for early builder projects vary but are generally less than the estimates above. As discussed more below, five early builders are constructing local or regional broadband networks for public safety. Some of these projects have begun construction and provided us with cost data. The new cell towers (and associated LTE equipment) for the regional network in the Los Angeles area average $196,000 per site. For equipment being attached to existing towers and sites, the average cost is $102,000. For the regional project in Adams County, Colorado, the cost per site is approximately $75,000. This cost reflects sites utilizing existing infrastructure that does not require strengthening. For budgetary purposes, the Adams County project has estimated the development of a new site at $500,000, an estimate that includes acquisition of land, tower construction, and utilities.[69]

As part of its planning and market research, FirstNet has developed a cost estimate for its public safety network that met most of the best practices against which we evaluated it. A reliable cost estimate is critical to the success of any program and is updated continually throughout its life cycle. Such an estimate provides the basis for informed investment decision making, realistic budget formulation and program resourcing, meaningful progress measurement, proactive course correction when warranted, and accountability for results. FirstNet's cost estimate, including the assumptions it is based on, are not public because of the highly sensitive nature of the information it contains. Based on our analysis of this estimate, using our *Cost Estimating and Assessment Guide*, we determined that FirstNet's cost estimate met the comprehensive, and substantially met the well-documented characteristics of a reliable cost estimate.[70] For example, we found that FirstNet's estimate completely defines the program (in this case, the public safety network), documents all cost-influencing assumptions, and documents calculations performed and estimating methodology used to derive each element's cost. We did not assess FirstNet's cost estimate against all the characteristics established in our *Cost Estimating and Assessment Guide*. Specifically, we did not assess whether FirstNet's estimate was "credible" or "accurate" because the estimate and its associated documentation were deemed business sensitive.[71] Therefore, we cannot say if the estimate is in line with the best practices associated with the credible and accurate characteristics of our *Cost Estimating and Assessment Guide*.[72]

Various Factors Will Influence Cost of FirstNet's Public Safety Network

Cost estimates notwithstanding, various factors will influence the cost of constructing and operating FirstNet's public safety network, including (1) the business model used, especially the extent of commercial partnerships; (2) use of existing infrastructure; (3) efforts to ensure network reliability; and (4) network coverage.

Extent of Commercial Partnerships

FirstNet's business model, especially the extent to which it partners with commercial carriers or other private enterprises, will influence the cost to construct and operate the public safety network. The 2012 act gives FirstNet the authority to engage in a variety of commercial partnerships.[73]

Such partnerships could involve a private-sector partner that would contribute resources to the network (e.g., infrastructure) and accept some risk in the form of profits or losses. FirstNet would then contribute other resources to the partnership (e.g., spectrum) conditioned on the network satisfying social objectives (i.e., enhancing public safety communications). In a partnership, public safety and commercial users could share the public safety network's infrastructure and spectrum, with public safety given priority to all network capacity during times of emergency. Regardless of the approach, some public safety stakeholders we spoke with maintained the need for FirstNet to work with commercial partners in building and operating the network for it to be financially sustainable. One study calculated that the value of serving both commercial and public safety users is greater than the costs of the additional capacity and signal reliability requirements placed on the network to serve both public safety and commercial users, demonstrating a strong business case for a public-private partnership.[74]

Use of Existing Infrastructure

The use of existing infrastructure will influence the cost to construct and operate FirstNet's public safety network. Under agreements to share existing wireless network infrastructure, FirstNet may be able to make use of, for example, cell towers, antennae, cabling, radio-processing equipment, backup power facilities, and the links between towers and the nearest communications hub, to the extent economically desirable to do so. According to FCC estimates, capital costs would be 2.5 times greater without this form of sharing. Given these potential financial savings, a few public safety stakeholders we spoke with maintained that FirstNet should use at least some existing infrastructure for the network. The use of existing infrastructure can have limitations though. For instance, using existing infrastructure can limit the design and coverage of the network, since existing towers and buildings can only facilitate certain network coverage given their physical location. Negotiating access to existing infrastructure can also be a time-consuming process, especially with government-owned or controlled facilities, and where contracts must by executed with multiple owners, ultimately slowing down network deployment. For example, when we spoke with Swedish officials about the public-safety communications network in their county, they said that they sought to use existing infrastructure, to save costs, when constructing their network, but faced problems in their largest cities convincing tower owners to allow the government to rent the towers.[75]

Furthermore, there is a risk when public safety entities rely on infrastructure owned by commercial operators, particularly if they have to rely on a single provider in any given location that can then charge high fees.

Efforts to Ensure Network Reliability

FirstNet's approach to ensure the public safety network is safe, secure, and resilient (that is, the overall reliability of the network) will also influence the cost to construct the network. FirstNet is required by the 2012 act to "ensure the safety, security, and resiliency of the network."[76]

FirstNet is still determining how it will satisfy this requirement.[77] As previously described, NPSTC published a report to provide guidance for FirstNet as it constructs and implements the public safety network.[78] NPSTC concluded that a "public-safety grade" communications system should be designed to resist failures due to manmade or natural events as much as practical, and that the public safety network must be constructed to meet as many of these requirements as possible. If FirstNet implements all of NPSTC's best practices, though, it will significantly add to the cost of building the network. For example, transmission sites, such as cell towers, should have backup power sources when used for public safety communications, according to NPSTC. Existing commercial sites, however, generally do not have such backup, primarily to reduce costs in extremely competitive markets. FCC, for instance, has reported that it could cost $35,000 per site to harden existing commercial LTE sites.[79]

Network Coverage

The public safety network's coverage will also influence the cost to construct and operate the network. The 2012 act requires FirstNet to establish a "nationwide" network, but does not define the level of coverage that constitutes "nationwide."[80] Generally speaking, increasing the area covered by the network, as well as the extent to which coverage penetrates buildings, increases the amount of infrastructure needed, and thus the cost of the network. It may be relatively affordable, for example, to cover large segments of the population concentrated in relatively small areas. For instance, one stakeholder we spoke with suggested that FirstNet could provide service to as much as 25 percent of all potential customers by covering just the 8 largest metropolitan areas. Providing coverage outside dense metropolitan areas can be particularly expensive. One study has shown that a nationwide public-safety broadband network would generally be profitable in urban areas and unprofitable in rural areas.[81] This study demonstrated that a network built with a commercial partnership could cover 94 percent of the U.S. population and break even because urban areas could subsidize coverage in rural areas.

FirstNet Faces Difficult Decisions about User Fees and Commercial Partnerships in Determining How to Become Self-Funding

Although FirstNet has various revenue options it is authorized to use to become self-funding, it is unclear how FirstNet will use those authorities. As the cost estimates discussed above illustrate, FirstNet's network will likely cost tens of billions of dollars to construct and initially operate. As also noted above, FirstNet is required to be self-funding. To meet the costs of building and maintaining the network, FirstNet may generate revenue through user fees and commercial partnerships, the latter of which can involve the secondary use of the network for non-public safety services. However, FirstNet faces difficult decisions determining how to best utilize these revenue sources. Additionally, regardless of the effectiveness of FirstNet's use of these revenue sources, the public safety network will likely have net negative income in the first few years of operation.[82]

User Fees

FirstNet can generate revenue through user fees, but the extent of this revenue will be determined by demand for the public safety network and other factors. According to stakeholders we spoke with and surveyed, demand for FirstNet's public safety network is significant. Many public safety entities we spoke with said that there is demand for a public-safety broadband network. Further, numerous SPOCs responding to our survey indicated that a public-safety broadband network will be very useful for public safety entities.[83] SPOCs we surveyed also noted that some public safety entities already use commercial wireless data services. Indeed, 80 percent of the SPOCs responded that law enforcement first responders who use commercial wireless data services use those services "always or often."[84] According to one SPOC, "the use of data for public safety is increasing rapidly and the existing commercial networks do not provide the necessary coverage or capacity." Another SPOC maintained that "theability to have reliable access to broadband data throughout the state would improve interoperability," as well as a first responder's ability to deliver critical services in a timely manner.

Despite the demand for the public safety network, a variety of challenges could hinder adoption and thus user fee revenue:

- **Fee size:** If FirstNet's user fee is too high it could hinder public safety adoption, and if it is too low it could bring in too little revenue. Numerous stakeholders we spoke with noted that FirstNet's cost would play a role in whether they adopt the public safety network and that user fees must be competitive with existing commercial services.[85] According to a few public safety entities we spoke with and the SPOCs we surveyed, public safety entities currently pay $20-$100 per user or device, per month, for commercial services.[86] While low user fees would be attractive to public safety entities and therefore may increase adoption, they would also bring in a relatively smaller amount of revenue per user.[87] As a FirstNet Senior Program Manager reported in December 2014, there is a trade-off with low user fees between adoption and the network's financial sustainability. Some stakeholders also noted that the cost of equipment and devices needed to access the public safety network could limit adoption, especially since public safety entities are continuing to invest in their LMR devices and equipment.
- **User base:** While a large user base can potentially bring in significant user fee revenue, it could be challenging to manage. The 2012 act

established that FirstNet's primary customers will be entities that provide "public safety services."[88] How FirstNet interprets the definitions of "public safety services" established in the 2012 act will expand or contract the potential sources of revenue.[89] As one public safety official we spoke with noted, the network has more value to public safety entities when there are more users on the network, because entities will all be able to communicate with each other. Another public safety official we spoke with suggested that certain users could be required to adopt the public safety network. Government users in Sweden, for instance, are required to pay a user fee, regardless of their use of the network, to generate revenue that is necessary to support the national network's maintenance and operations. However, a large user base can require priority and preemption rules, if certain users are to have privileged access to the network. According to some public safety officials we spoke with, such rules can be difficult to establish among public safety entities.

- **Coverage:** Widespread network coverage can attract more users, and thus user fee revenue, but is expensive to construct and maintain. As the FirstNet Senior Program Manager reported in December 2014, there is a trade-off with increased coverage between adoption and the network's financial sustainability. Further, FirstNet does not have total control over the network's coverage, since states may opt out and build their own RANs. Nevertheless, some of the public safety entities we spoke with said that the network's coverage would play a role in whether they adopt the public safety network, noting in particular that the coverage should be at least as good as existing commercial services. One public safety entity we spoke with said that existing commercial coverage is inadequate, while two other entities said that the coverage is adequate normally, but the service becomes unusable during large events because of the number of users on the network. However, as noted above, providing extensive coverage, especially in rural areas, can be very costly. Indeed, a few SPOCs noted in survey responses that providing rural coverage in their states would be challenging, with one commenting that "it is inconceivable that FirstNet will be able to deploy a terrestrial network in the vast areas that are unpopulated or sparsely populated."
- **Reliability:** Although FirstNet is required to construct a resilient network, practices to ensure this can be costly. Some public safety officials we spoke with said that the network's reliability would play a

> role in whether they adopt the public safety network. A few officials specifically said that if the network did not reliably work when first utilized by public safety, adoption would suffer, since public safety has a low tolerance for unreliable technology. However, as noted above, ensuring reliability requires significant capital expenses. As the FirstNet Senior Program Manager reported in December 2014, there is also a trade-off with hardening the network between the extent of adoption and the network's financial sustainability.

Compounding these challenges are other factors that might hinder adoption. For instance, officials from some public safety entities told us that public safety tends to take a "wait and see" approach to adopting new technology. Public safety, according to an official we spoke with, can be reluctant to buy and use new technology and services because if those things do not work it can put lives in jeopardy. Furthermore, according to officials from two public safety entities we spoke with, some entities may not see a need for a nationwide public-safety network if they operate in areas with few large-scale emergencies.

Commercial Partnerships

FirstNet can also generate revenue through commercial partnerships, but the extent of commercial interest in these partnerships, and therefore the value of this authority for FirstNet, is currently unknown.[90] Under the 2012 act, FirstNet can receive payment for the use of the public safety network's capacity by non-public safety users as well as use of the network's infrastructure.[91] The value of secondary access to the public safety network's capacity depends in part on the availability of the spectrum, which itself will be determined in part by the capacity available given the network's design. According to one major carrier we spoke with, no business is likely to enter into a partnership with FirstNet because its public-safety user base has not been defined, and thus the network's capacity available to secondary (commercial) users is unknown.

According to this carrier, the risk would be too high for a commercial entity to enter into an agreement without knowing exactly how they will be able to use FirstNet's network. If public safety preempts all commercial traffic, then the commercial entity will struggle to generate income from this venture and may lose favor with its customers. However, another major carrier we spoke with maintained that FirstNet will have to partner with at least one commercial carrier to be financially sustainable, and given the significant investments in LTE infrastructure made by commercial carriers, FirstNet would do well to utilize some of this infrastructure through commercial partnerships. Although the historic Advanced Wireless Services spectrum auction that FCC concluded in late January 2015 could indicate demand for spectrum capacity among commercial carriers,[92] the extent of carrier interest in partnering with FirstNet is not yet fully known. In particular, there may be some benefits to existing commercial carriers in partnering with FirstNet, but these companies may prefer to expand their businesses by directly competing with FirstNet and offering their own public safety products. Notably, when FCC presented the D Block spectrum for auction in 2008 with public safety encumbrances, it received no qualifying bids and thus the D Block was not licensed. The lack of commercial interest in the D Block was due in part to uncertainty about how the public-private partnership would work, which raises further questions about FirstNet's ability to partner with commercial carriers.[93]

ALTHOUGH EARLY BUILDER PROJECTS ARE PROVIDING LESSONS, FIRSTNET HAS NOT DEVELOPED A PLAN TO EVALUATE THEM

Early Builder Projects Have Learned Lessons As They Develop Public Safety Networks

Officials from the five early builder projects, as well as the three canceled projects, told us that they have learned a number of lessons while developing their public-safety broadband networks that may be useful as FirstNet develops its public safety network. Specifically, the early builders identified lessons about (1) governance, (2) financing the network, (3) conducting outreach, and (4) planning for network deployment.

Governance

Officials from the early builder projects cited governance lessons associated with developing a new network for public safety. As we reported in February 2012, governance is a key element for interoperable networks.[94] By providing a framework for collaboration and decision making with the goal of achieving a common objective, governance structures can promote interoperability and help ensure public safety networks are secure and reliable. The 2012 act established FirstNet as the governing entity for a nationwide public-safety network, and as such, early builder project officials described governance challenges that FirstNet may face. For example, officials from one project told us some public safety entities may not have a clear understanding of FirstNet's goals and plans. The officials told us localities are willing to participate in the public safety network, but FirstNet will face difficulty in establishing timely technical decisions and effective policies that keep pace with local enthusiasm to participate. The officials said FirstNet can address this challenge by setting expectations about what the network will provide, including the specific intent, purpose, and planned capabilities. A SPOC working with one of the projects described challenges that FirstNet will face in determining how to diplomatically work with tribal nations. For example, whereas each state will have a designated SPOC, tribes are sovereign nations within a state but will not have a designated SPOC, which could pose governance challenges. The SPOC told us it is unclear whether FirstNet has planned for how the "opt in" or "opt out" process will work for tribal nations, when the 2012 act requires state governors to make the state decision. The SPOC also told us that a tribe representative in his state met with him to share concerns about how public safety entities only have broadband coverage near the edge of their reservation's limits. The SPOC noted that the tribe has become a partner of the early builder project and that this partnership underscores how their state has developed close relationships with tribes through state-level liaison efforts, federal grant programs, and its early builder project. According to the SPOC, FirstNet should work closely with states and leverage these relationships to work with tribal nations.

Financing the Network

Officials from the early builder projects also learned lessons related to financing a new public safety network that could be applicable to FirstNet. Although the 2012 act provides FirstNet with funding sources and options, as described above, utilizing such sources could be challenging according to early builder project stakeholders. Officials from a project told us they will face sustainability challenges due to the limited number of users that will be able to utilize their network. According to the officials, their project will not be able to charge their users enough to make the operations sustainable without pricing the users out of the services. The officials told us a possible way to address this challenge would be to expand the service to public safety entities in neighboring metropolitan areas and airport services areas that have established broadband infrastructure. Similarly, officials from one of the projects said their network will be in an "uneasy" financial position initially because the number of users subscribing to the network will likely be low. Further, the officials noted that a small user base could make it difficult to maintain the network because user fees are expected to pay for a significant portion of network operations and maintenance. According to a SPOC working with one of the projects, determining user fees to cover ongoing maintenance and administrative costs has been a financial challenge. To decide user fees, project officials are considering factors including the potential for public-private partnerships and how to define the scope of the user base. As we found in February 2012, obtaining adequate funds to build, operate, and maintain a public safety network could be challenging.[95]

Conducting Outreach

Early builder project officials cited lessons they learned for conducting outreach while developing their public safety networks. According to project officials, effectively conducting outreach as required by the 2012 act could be challenging for FirstNet. According to officials working with one of the projects, network coverage will be a challenging outreach topic and FirstNet must be prepared to explain the coverage strategy for each state. The officials said most public safety officials in their state are aware that network coverage is typically provided through a myriad of approaches such as permanent infrastructure, mobile "deployables," and satellites.[96] However, the officials noted, until FirstNet sets clear and valid expectations on those approaches, state stakeholders for the public safety network will face difficulty holding constructive conversations about which coverage solutions are the most feasible. Another SPOC described challenges in their state on the topic of network coverage. According to the SPOC, their state's public safety community and tribal nations became frustrated with FirstNet's inconsistent messaging about the network's coverage and capability. The inconsistent messaging created challenges for the SPOC in convincing frustrated potential users to remain engaged in the state's FirstNet planning efforts. We also spoke with a SPOC closely involved in one of the early builder projects who described strategies that his state's project used in conducting outreach. For example, the project developed contact lists for each site deployment location and for primary and secondary stakeholders, and distributed materials in public safety locations including police stations. According to the SPOC, FirstNet will need to sustain a level of excitement in its outreach for the public safety network.

Planning for Network Deployment

Officials from the early builder projects as well as the canceled public-safety projects also described lessons they learned about planning their network's deployment that could benefit FirstNet. Officials from one project told us they learned specific lessons about site selection, permits and site access agreements, and equipment choices. The officials also told us they selected the RFP response that was the most economical in its use of existing infrastructure.

Officials from another project told us how they chose to deploy in densely populated areas with high-crime rates, where public safety coordination is typically challenging and in most need of improvement. The officials also said they provided guidance to local police departments that helped them avoid procuring communications devices that would not be compatible with the project or FirstNet's public safety network. An official from one of the canceled projects said his team faced several challenges including local zoning conditions that affected project schedule and cost, a newly passed city code that required towers to withstand higher wind loads and that increased costs, and commercial competitors lowering their subscription rates to compete with the planned public-safety network.

Officials from an ongoing project told us their project initially identified "buildout" sites but learned that environmental assessments would need to be completed for each site. Doing these assessments would threaten the project's ability to follow its project schedule. To address the challenge, the project narrowed its buildout site pool to exclude marshlands and other areas with obstructive tree lines and to include publicly owned sites such as police and fire stations. With the publicly owned sites identified, project officials worked with their state's legislature to pass an exemption to state environmental reviews.

According to a SPOC we spoke with, the project's efforts on this issue will reduce the project's overall build time. The official from the project told us that an important lesson learned is to thoroughly understand all of the process steps and risks prior to plan execution. According to the project official, it will be important for FirstNet to be able to navigate similar issues and challenges.

FirstNet Has Processes in Place to Identify Early Builder Project Lessons but Has Not Developed a Written Evaluation Plan

While FirstNet has taken steps to collect and evaluate lessons learned from the early builder projects, it could do more to ensure that the lessons are properly evaluated.

We have previously found that a well-developed evaluation plan for projects like the early builder projects can help ensure that agencies obtain the information necessary to make effective program and policy decisions.[97] A well-developed evaluation plan should include, at a minimum, several key features including the following:

- well-defined, clear, and measurable objectives;
- criteria or standards for determining project performance;
- a clear plan that details the type and source of data necessary to evaluate the project, methods for data collection, and timing and frequency of data collection; and
- a detailed data-analysis plan to track performance and evaluate the projects' final results.

FirstNet has taken steps to identify objectives and standards for early builder project performance, as well as the data and information it will collect from the early builder projects. As noted above, FirstNet entered into SMLAs with the early builder projects that permit their use of FirstNet's spectrum. Under the SMLAs, the early builders agreed to conduct specific activities on their networks, also known as key-learning conditions, and develop a Key Learning Conditions Plan with FirstNet in exchange for spectrum use.[98] Under the plans, early builder projects will submit various deliverables to FirstNet, such as project plans and schedules, as well as documentation describing the project's specific procedures and experiences.[99] According to a SPOC involved in one of the projects, FirstNet's key-learning conditions cover a comprehensive set of issues and should provide valuable data for FirstNet. Under the SMLAs, the projects also agree to provide FirstNet with quarterly reporting on their project's use of FirstNet's spectrum, progress achieving project milestones, and in some cases, the experiences of their network users. In October 2014.

FirstNet provided the projects with quarterly report templates, instructions, and timing for completing the reports. Additionally, FirstNet intends to gain knowledge from the projects through contractors who have been assigned to each project to provide information and collect formal and informal lessons.[100]

FirstNet told us the contractors are using an informal lessons log to track observed lessons and whether they have been incorporated into the technical documents used to guide FirstNet's acquisition of a comprehensive network solution. FirstNet officials also told us that they hold weekly meetings to review early builder project status, progress on SMLA key-learning conditions, and informal key lessons. Finally, in April 2014 FirstNet authorized the PSAC to establish an Early Builder Working Group to provide advice on the strategies and lessons learned related to the early builder network development, outreach, and consultation. As of January 2015, the PSAC planned to submit the Early Builder Working Group's first series of recommendations to FirstNet.

Although FirstNet has taken these steps, we are concerned that it lacks a detailed data-analysis plan to track the performance and results of the early builder projects. For the early builder projects, their performance and results are captured in the observations and lessons learned reported to FirstNet and identified by consultants. Tracking the early builder projects' observations and lessons against FirstNet technical documentation is necessary to ensure that the lessons have been addressed and also facilitates transparency and accountability for FirstNet's decision-making. Even though FirstNet staff and contractors remain in close contact with the early builder projects, without a data- analysis plan to track those projects it is unclear how FirstNet intends to evaluate the projects' observations and lessons and determine whether or how the lessons are addressed. As a result, we believe that FirstNet could miss opportunities to leverage key lessons related to governance, finance, outreach, and network deployment. Given that the early builder projects are doing, in part, on a regional and local level what FirstNet must eventually do on a national level, a complete evaluation plan that includes a detailed data-analysis plan could play a key role in FirstNet's strategic planning and program management, providing feedback on both program design and execution. Furthermore, such a plan could provide FirstNet officials the opportunity to make informed midcourse changes as they plan for the public safety network, and help ensure that lessons from these projects are evaluated in ways that generate reliable information to inform future program-development decisions.

CONCLUSION

The lack of interoperability in public safety communications has been a long-standing concern given the essential role these communications play in protecting lives, health, and property. The 2012 act provided FirstNet with the basic resources necessary—such as spectrum and initial capital—to establish an interoperable broadband network for all public safety entities. However, there is no guarantee that FirstNet will be able to successfully develop and operate this nationwide network. FirstNet is tasked with a complex and challenging mission to establish the network, which researchers have estimated could cost as much as $47 billion to construct and operate over its first 10 years.

Furthermore, FirstNet faces a multitude of risks, significant challenges, and difficult decisions in meeting its statutory responsibilities, including determining how to become a self-funding entity. If FirstNet fails to generate enough revenue to operate the network over the long-term, for example, it could jeopardize the existence of this new public safety network. At this time, the extent to which FirstNet can generate revenue through partnerships with commercial carriers remains unknown, especially given that some commercial carriers could choose to compete with FirstNet. However, FirstNet is taking certain actions to help ensure that its public safety network is successful. For instance, to date it has effectively consulted with stakeholders and maintained a rigorous cost estimate.

Although FirstNet has started to establish an internal control system to help it meet its statutory responsibilities, we found FirstNet could strengthen its internal controls. In particular, while FirstNet has begun taking some steps to assess risks, it has not fully assessed the risks it faces. Complete risk assessments would help FirstNet respond to risks in a proactive manner and make the best use of its resources by appropriately responding to the most pressing risks. FirstNet could also strengthen its internal controls by fully establishing its control environment, which is the foundation for an effective internal control system. Currently, FirstNet has not established a cohesive standards of conduct policy, which means FirstNet may not be able to address deviations in conduct and performance and take corrective actions in a timely manner. Establishing and evaluating adherence to standards of conduct would help FirstNet ensure that all its personnel are held accountable for their actions and foster stakeholder trust in FirstNet's ability to meet its statutory responsibilities.

Early builder projects have learned important lessons related to governance, finance, outreach, and network deployment that could be useful to FirstNet as it develops its plans to establish a nationwide network. However, FirstNet lacks a detailed data-analysis plan to track the projects' observations and lessons learned. Without such a plan, it is unclear how FirstNet intends to evaluate the early builder projects and ensure that the lessons have been addressed and incorporated, if applicable, into FirstNet's planning. As a result, FirstNet could miss opportunities to leverage the key lessons the projects learned. A complete evaluation plan for the early builder projects that includes a detailed data-analysis plan would increase transparency and help FirstNet's strategic planning and program management, which are important given the complexity of FirstNet's mission.

Furthermore, such a plan would provide FirstNet officials the opportunity to make informed midcourse changes as they plan the nationwide network and help ensure that lessons from these projects are evaluated in ways that generate reliable information to inform future network-deployment decisions.

Recommendations for Executive Action

To improve the accountability and transparency of FirstNet's operations, and ensure that FirstNet is gaining as much knowledge from the early builder projects as possible, we recommend that FirstNet take the following two actions:

- strengthen FirstNet's internal control system by fully assessing risks, developing standards of conduct, and evaluating performance against these standards, and
- develop an evaluation plan that includes a detailed data-analysis plan for the early builder projects' performance and results, including how the observations and lessons learned reported to FirstNet and identified by consultants will be evaluated.

Agency Comments

We provided a draft of this report to the Departments of Commerce and Homeland Security, FCC, and FirstNet for their review and comment.

The Department of Commerce and FirstNet provided written comments DHS, FCC, FirstNet, and NTIA (within the Department of Commerce), provided technical comments that we incorporated as appropriate.

In its written comments, the Department of Commerce stressed that it takes its oversight responsibilities with respect to FirstNet seriously, is committed to the success of the public-safety broadband network, and supports the response provided to us from FirstNet. In its written comments, FirstNet stated that it agreed with all of our recommendations and noted activities that it will undertake to implement them. Regarding strengthening internal controls,

FirstNet stated that it is cognizant that, as a newly formed government entity, it must continue its efforts to establish comprehensive internal control policies and procedures. FirstNet reiterated that it has initiated a legal compliance risk assessment focusing on key legal risk areas and stated that it will also undertake a full risk assessment. FirstNet also stated that it plans to establish supplemental standards of conduct, which will operate in conjunction with applicable regulations and existing FirstNet and Department of Commerce policies. Regarding an evaluation plan for lessons learned from the early builder projects, FirstNet stated that it will develop an appropriate evaluation plan consistent with the principles we specified. FirstNet noted that it has already enacted a standard operating procedure that ensures information and lessons from the projects are appropriately distributed within FirstNet, and it will use this process to disseminate the findings gathered under the evaluation plan.

Sincerely yours,

Mark L. Goldstein
Director, Physical Infrastructure

APPENDIX I: OBJECTIVES, SCOPE, AND METHODOLOGY

This report examines the First Responder Network Authority (FirstNet) and its progress towards establishing a nationwide public-safety broadband network (hereafter, the public safety network). Specifically, we reviewed (1) the extent to which FirstNet is carrying out its responsibilities and establishing internal controls for developing the public safety network, (2) how much the public safety network is estimated to cost to construct and operate and how

FirstNet plans to become a self-funding entity, and (3) what lessons can be learned from local and regional public-safety network projects.

To determine the extent to which FirstNet is carrying out its responsibilities and establishing internal controls, we reviewed FirstNet documentation and conducted interviews. We reviewed all of FirstNet's Requests for Information, Notices, and annual reports to Congress. We also reviewed relevant board-meeting materials and resolutions, presentations to stakeholders, press releases and blog posts, and other documentation. We interviewed and received written responses from FirstNet, the National Telecommunications and Information Administration, and Department of Commerce officials to obtain further information on their efforts. We compared FirstNet's efforts and progress carrying out its responsibilities against requirements established in the Middle Class Tax Relief and Job Creation Act of 2012 (2012 act).[101] However, we did not review FirstNet's progress against every responsibility established for it in the 2012 act, because it is not possible for FirstNet to have made progress on some responsibilities. For instance, FirstNet cannot develop terms of service for the use of the public safety network without first developing the network, the design of which is itself dependent on consultation with a wide variety of stakeholders. We did compare FirstNet's efforts establishing internal controls against criteria established in the federal *Standards for Internal Control*.[102] For the scope of this review, we chose to evaluate FirstNet's policies and practices against the first two components of internal control: control environment and risk assessment.

We chose these two components because the control environment is the foundation for an internal control system and risk assessment provides the basis for developing appropriate risk responses and control activities. We also assessed FirstNet's outreach efforts against core principles for effective stakeholder participation identified by our previous reports.[103] Further, as described below, we interviewed a variety of public safety officials about their perspectives on FirstNet's progress to date.

To learn how much the public safety network is estimated to cost and how FirstNet plans to become self-funding, we reviewed cost estimates from FirstNet and others, and conducted interviews. Specifically, we reviewed cost estimates for nationwide public-safety broadband networks from a variety of entities, including the Congressional Budget Office, the Federal Communications Commission (FCC), and academics. We identified these cost estimates through interviews with agency officials and subject matter experts.

We did not perform a full data reliability assessment of the numbers in these estimates because the purpose of the estimates within the scope of our review was to provide illustrative examples. We also reviewed FirstNet's cost estimate. We used our *Cost Estimating and Assessment Guide*, which is based on research of best practices, to estimate program schedules and costs.[104] Due to the procurement sensitivity of the estimate, we assessed FirstNet's cost estimate against two of the characteristics of reliable cost estimates: comprehensive and well-documented.[105] Our *Cost Guide* considers an estimate to be comprehensive if its level of detail ensures that all pertinent costs are included and that no costs are double-counted, and that costs are well documented in order that the estimate can be easily repeated or updated and can be traced to original sources through auditing. We also interviewed members of FirstNet's cost-estimating team to obtain a detailed understanding of the cost model, such as how it was prepared, the assumptions underlying it, and the documentation supporting it. We also interviewed FirstNet officials about how it plans to become self- funding.

To assess the factors that will influence the cost of the public safety network and challenges FirstNet may face in becoming self-funding, we conducted a variety of interviews and reviewed documents. As described below, we interviewed officials involved in early builder projects, as well as state and local public-safety entities. We also interviewed subject matter experts who were interviewed for our previous report on emergency communications. Additionally, we interviewed two major commercial wireless carriers for their perspectives on building and operating a public safety network. We also reviewed FirstNet documentation, academic literature suggested to us by subject matter experts, and reports published by FCC and the National Public Safety Telecommunications Council (NPSTC).[106]

To identify lessons that can be learned from local and regional public-safety broadband network early builder projects, we interviewed project officials and reviewed documentation from FirstNet and the projects. Specifically, we conducted site visits and phone interviews with officials from—and involved in—the five current projects (Los Angeles, CA; Adams County, CO; New Jersey; New Mexico; and Harris County, TX), the three projects that were canceled (Charlotte, NC; Mississippi; and San Francisco, CA), and state and local public-safety entities in the project jurisdictions. We also reviewed the Spectrum Manager Lease Agreements that each of the five current projects established with FirstNet, and documentation related to how FirstNet plans to collect lessons learned from the projects, such as Key Learning Condition Plans, project quarterly reporting requirements, and other documentation provided by project officials. We also interviewed and obtained written responses from FirstNet officials to obtain more information about their plans to evaluate and utilize lessons from the projects. We assessed FirstNet's plans to evaluate and utilize lessons from the projects against key features of a well-developed evaluation plan for pilot projects identified by our previous reports.[107]

Finally, to obtain stakeholder views on all our objectives, we surveyed all 50 states, the District of Columbia, and 5 U.S. territories and conducted interviews.[108] We emailed the survey to the Single Point of Contact (SPOC); we obtained the list of SPOCs from FirstNet's website. The survey included questions about demand for the public safety network and SPOCs' satisfaction with FirstNet's progress and consultation efforts, among other things. To ensure that our survey questions and skip pattern were clear and logical and that respondents could answer the questions without undue burden, we pretested our survey with four states: Maryland, Mississippi, Montana, and New Jersey. We selected the pretest states in order to provide for variation in level of engagement and experience with public-safety broadband networks and FirstNet, and geographic location. We administered the survey from October 2014 through November 2014; therefore, responses reflect information and views as of that time. We received 55 responses, for a 98 percent response rate. Puerto Rico did not respond to our survey. We also interviewed a variety of stakeholders, such as state and local public- safety entities, commercial wireless carriers, subject matter experts, public safety associations, and other federal agencies, such as FCC and the Department of Homeland Security. We also spoke with government officials in Sweden responsible for establishing a public-safety communications network in their country. We selected stakeholders by considering their involvement in early builder jurisdictions, experience with operating and using wireless communications systems and public safety-communications systems and devices in particular, familiarity with FirstNet and its mission, and—to obtain a cross-section of public safety disciplines—their public safety role.[109] Among public safety entities, we interviewed seven law enforcement, four fire, three emergency medical service, three emergency management or communications, and two general public safety entities.

Appendix II: Copy of Survey to FirstNet Single Points of Contact

GAO United States Government Accountability Office

FirstNet State Survey

Introduction

The U.S. Government Accountability Office (GAO) is an agency that gathers and analyzes information for the Congress. The Ranking Member of the Committee on Commerce, Science, and Transportation, U.S. Senate, has asked GAO to examine the First Responder Network Authority (FirstNet), including how it is carrying out its responsibilities related to the establishment of a nationwide public safety broadband network. As part of our review, we are, among other things, surveying all FirstNet State Single Points of Contact (SPOC). Results from this survey will help inform Congress about FirstNet's progress to date, challenges it may face, and the efforts of states to help establish the nationwide public safety broadband network. We plan to issue a report to the Congress in the spring of 2015.

In our report to Congress, we will generally use only the aggregated results of this survey. While we may use individual responses, we will not attribute them to individual respondents in our report or otherwise disclose them to the public. GAO will not disclose such information, unless required by law or requested by Congress.

Please answer the questions in this survey from your perspective as a SPOC and to the best of your knowledge. In this survey, references to a nationwide public safety broadband network refer to a fully operational network established by FirstNet. Additionally, in this survey, by "state" we mean any state or territory and the District of Columbia. If you are not able to answer all the questions in this survey yourself, please forward this survey or coordinate your responses with the appropriate people to the extent possible. At the end of the survey, you will have an opportunity to expand upon any of your responses and provide any additional comments you may have.

Please complete this survey within 2 weeks of receiving it. In testing this survey, we found that it took approximately 45 minutes to complete. We may contact you to clarify responses as needed.

Thank you in advance for your time and participation.

GAO Contacts

If you have any questions about this GAO survey, please contact:

Sally Moino at (214) 777-5610 (moinos@gao.gov)
Or
Nalylee Padilla at (202) 512-6797 (padillan@gao.gov)

Demand for a Nationwide Public Safety Broadband Network

1. Generally, how useful will a public safety broadband network be for the following public safety entities in your state?

	Very useful	Moderately useful	Not useful	Don't know	Not applicable	No response
a. Emergency Management	☐	☐	☐	☐	☐	☐
b. Emergency Medical Services	☐	☐	☐	☐	☐	☐
c. Federal Public Safety Entities	☐	☐	☐	☐	☐	☐
d. Fire Services						
e. Law Enforcement	☐	☐	☐	☐	☐	☐
f. Public Works	☐	☐	☐	☐	☐	☐
g. Tribal Public Safety Entities	☐	☐	☐	☐	☐	☐
h. Other Potential Users (specify):						
______________	☐	☐	☐	☐	☐	☐

1a. Please provide any additional comments or explanations you have on the usefulness of a public safety broadband network to public safety entities in your state.

2. About how many first responders from the following public safety entities in your state are using commercial wireless data services?

	Most	Some	Few	None	Don't know	Not applicable	No response
a. Emergency Management	☐	☐	☐	☐	☐	☐	☐
b. Emergency Medical Services	☐	☐	☐	☐	☐	☐	☐
c. Federal Public Safety Entities	☐	☐	☐	☐	☐	☐	☐
d. Fire Services	☐	☐	☐	☐	☐	☐	☐
e. Law Enforcement	☐	☐	☐	☐	☐	☐	☐
f. Public Works	☐	☐	☐	☐	☐	☐	☐
g. Tribal Public Safety Entities	☐	☐	☐	☐	☐	☐	☐
h. Other Potential Users (specify):							
______________	☐	☐	☐	☐	☐	☐	☐

3. Among first responders who use commercial wireless data services in your state, how frequently do they use those services?

	Always or Often	Sometimes	Rarely or Never	Don't know	Not applicable	No response
a. Emergency Management	☐	☐	☐	☐	☐	☐
b. Emergency Medical Services	☐	☐	☐	☐	☐	☐
c. Federal Public Safety Entities	☐	☐	☐	☐	☐	☐
d. Fire Services	☐	☐	☐	☐	☐	☐
e. Law Enforcement	☐	☐	☐	☐	☐	☐
f. Public Works	☐	☐	☐	☐	☐	☐
g. Tribal Public Safety Entities	☐	☐	☐	☐	☐	☐
h. Other Potential Users (specify): ______________	☐	☐	☐	☐	☐	☐

4. What is the typical cost per month, per subscriber, for commercial wireless data services used by first responders in your state?

FirstNet Responsibilities

The questions in this section ask about your satisfaction with FirstNet's progress carrying out its responsibilities (as established in Title VI of the Middle Class Tax Relief and Job Creation Act of 2012). Specifically, the questions ask about your satisfaction with FirstNet's progress on developing and designing a secure and reliable nationwide public safety broadband network.

5. How satisfied or dissatisfied are you with FirstNet's progress to date on each of the following responsibilities?

	Very satisfied	Moderately satisfied	Neither satisfied nor dissatisfied	Moderately dissatisfied	Very dissatisfied	Don't know enough about FirstNet's progress	No response
a. Hire FirstNet staff	☐	☐	☐	☐	☐	☐	☐
b. Develop the technical and operational requirements of the network	☐	☐	☐	☐	☐	☐	☐
c. Develop the practices, procedures, and standards for managing and operating the network	☐	☐	☐	☐	☐	☐	☐
d. Develop service-level agreements for use of the network	☐	☐	☐	☐	☐	☐	☐
e. Carry out a transparent Request for Information process	☐	☐	☐	☐	☐	☐	☐
f. Issue open, transparent, and competitive Requests for Proposals	☐	☐	☐	☐	☐	☐	☐
g. Promote integration of the network with Next Generation 911 (NG911)	☐	☐	☐	☐	☐	☐	☐
h. Consult with state public safety entities on the development of the network	☐	☐	☐	☐	☐	☐	☐
i. Consult with local public safety entities on the development of the network	☐	☐	☐	☐	☐	☐	☐
j. Consult with tribal public safety entities on the development of the network	☐	☐	☐	☐	☐	☐	☐

6. Please provide any additional comments you have on FirstNet's progress carrying out its responsibilities and your level of satisfaction with that progress.

7. What obstacles, if any, has FirstNet faced, or may it face, due to its placement within the National Telecommunications and Information Administration (which is a component of the U.S. Department of Commerce)?

State Governance and Outreach

8. Does your state have a governance structure established to work with FirstNet?

Yes ☐
No ☐
Don't know ☐
No response ☐

8a. If you responded No, please explain in the box below.

9. Does your state have an outreach plan to educate your state's public safety entities about FirstNet and the nationwide public safety broadband network?

Yes ☐
No ☐
Don't know ☐
No response ☐

9a. If you responded No, please explain in the box below.

10. What special or unique circumstances may create challenges for deploying, operating, or maintaining the nationwide public safety broadband network in your state?

FirstNet Consultation with States

11. Has your state had its consultation meeting with FirstNet?

Yes.................. ☐

No.................. ☐

Don't know......... ☐

No response......... ☐

11a. If your state has not yet had its consultation meeting with FirstNet, but one is scheduled, please indicate the meeting date in the box below.

12. To what extent has FirstNet sought input from your state on the following aspects of the nationwide public safety broadband network?

	Not at all	To a small extent	To a moderate extent	To a large extent	Don't know	No response
a. Design and construction of the core network	☐	☐	☐	☐	☐	☐
b. Design and construction of the radio access network	☐	☐	☐	☐	☐	☐
c. Coverage area(s)	☐	☐	☐	☐	☐	☐
d. Hardening, reliability, and resiliency requirements	☐	☐	☐	☐	☐	☐
e. Security requirements	☐	☐	☐	☐	☐	☐
f. Eligible users	☐	☐	☐	☐	☐	☐
g. Priority access amongst public safety entities	☐	☐	☐	☐	☐	☐
h. Training needs of users	☐	☐	☐	☐	☐	☐
i. User fee pricing	☐	☐	☐	☐	☐	☐
j. Mission critical voice communications capabilities	☐	☐	☐	☐	☐	☐
k. Community resistance to network infrastructure	☐	☐	☐	☐	☐	☐

13. How much more, if at all, should FirstNet focus on the following aspects of the nationwide public safety broadband network in its outreach to your state?

	Stay the same	Slight increase	Moderate increase	Large increase	Don't know	No response
a. Design and construction of the core network	☐	☐	☐	☐	☐	☐
b. Design and construction of the radio access network	☐	☐	☐	☐	☐	☐
c. Coverage area(s)	☐	☐	☐	☐	☐	☐
d. Hardening, reliability, and resiliency requirements	☐	☐	☐	☐	☐	☐
e. Security requirements	☐	☐	☐	☐	☐	☐
f. Eligible users	☐	☐	☐	☐	☐	☐
g. Priority access amongst public safety entities	☐	☐	☐	☐	☐	☐
h. Training needs of users	☐	☐	☐	☐	☐	☐
i. User fee pricing	☐	☐	☐	☐	☐	☐
j. Mission critical voice communications capabilities	☐	☐	☐	☐	☐	☐
k. Community resistance to network infrastructure	☐	☐	☐	☐	☐	☐

14. Please provide any comments you have on the above aspects of the nationwide public safety broadband network.

15. How satisfied or dissatisfied are you with FirstNet's overall level of consultation, coordination, and communication with your state, including the level of input FirstNet has sought from your state?

Very satisfied.......................... ☐

Moderately satisfied.................. ☐

Neither satisfied nor dissatisfied... ☐

Moderately dissatisfied............... ☐

Very dissatisfied........................ ☐

Don't know............................. ☐

No response............................ ☐

16. Has FirstNet provided your state with information or guidance related to its nationwide public safety broadband network to make decisions in your state?

Yes, just enough information ☐

Yes, but would like more information ☐

No, need more information ☐

Don't know ☐

No response ☐

17. Please provide any additional comments you have on FirstNet's consultation and outreach in your state.

18. What factors, if any, would influence your state's decision to opt-out of the nationwide public safety broadband network?

19. If you would like to expand upon any of your responses to the questions above, or have any other comments about FirstNet and the nationwide public safety broadband network, please write them in the box below.

End Notes

[1] Pub. L. No. 112-96, 126 Stat. 156 (2012).

[2] Pub. L. No. 112-96, § 6204(a), 126 Stat. 156, 208.

[3] The radio frequency spectrum is the part of the natural spectrum of electromagnetic radiation lying between the frequency limits of 3 kilohertz (kHz) and 300 gigahertz (GHz). Radio frequencies are grouped into bands. Radio signals travel through space in the form of

waves. These waves vary in length, and each wavelength is associated with a particular radio frequency.

[4] Pub. L. No. 112-96, § 6206(b)(2)(B), 126 Stat. 156, 212.

[5] GAO, *Emergency Communications: Various Challenges Likely to Slow Implementation of a Public Safety Broadband Network*, GAO-12-343 (Washington, D.C.: Feb. 22, 2012).

[6] Pub. L. No. 112-96, § 6206(c)(2)(A), 126 Stat. 156, 213.

[7] Pub. L. No. 112-96, 126 Stat. 156.

[8] GAO, *Standards for Internal Control in the Federal Government*, GAO/AIMD-00-21.3.1 (Washington, D.C.: Nov. 1999). The most recent version of these standards was issued in September 2014. GAO, *Standards for Internal Control in the Federal Government*, GAO-14-704G (Washington, D.C.: Sept. 10, 2014). These new standards become effective October 1, 2015, but an entity's management may elect early adoption.

According to FirstNet officials, as the Department of Commerce proceeds with the rollout of these revisions, NTIA and FirstNet will also adopt these new standards. Although these new standards are not yet effective and FirstNet is not required to abide by them, given that they will be effective soon and that FirstNet is still in the process of developing its internal control system, doing so according to these new standards would prevent FirstNet from having to re-design any elements of its system later this year.

[9] We did not perform a full data reliability assessment of the numbers in these estimates because the purpose of the estimates within the scope of our review was to provide illustrative examples.

[10] GAO, *GAO Cost Estimating and Assessment Guide: Best Practices for Developing and Managing Capital Program Costs*, GAO-09-3SP (Washington, D.C.: Mar. 2, 2009).

[11] See, for example, GAO, *Tax Administration: IRS Needs to Strengthen Its Approach for Evaluating the SRFMI Data-Sharing Pilot Program*, GAO-09-45 (Washington, D.C.: Nov. 7, 2008).

[12] Puerto Rico did not respond to our survey.

[13] We conducted semi-structured interviews with all of these stakeholders and throughout this report we refer to "a few" of the stakeholders if officials from 3-5 entities, "some" if 6-9, "many" if 10-14, and "numerous" if 15 or more expressed the view.

[14] Pub. L. No. 112-96, § 6208(a)(1). Also, under Section 6208(a)(2) of the act, FirstNet is allowed to establish agreements that allow access to the public safety network through entities involved in the construction, management, or operation of the public safety network, on a secondary basis for services other than public safety, such as individual commercial customers using the network much as they currently use existing commercial networks.

[15] Pub. L. No. 112-96, § 6202(b), 126 Stat, 156, 206.

[16] "Backhaul" is the telecommunications industry term that refers to connections between a central telecommunications network and other nodes outside the central network, such as a cell phone tower.

[17] Pub. L. No. 112-96, § 6204(b)(2)(B), 126 Stat. 156, 209.

[18] Pub. L. No. 112-96, § 6205, 126 Stat. 156, 211.

[19] Pub. L. No. 112-96, § 6206(c)(2)(B), 126 Stat. 156, 214.

[20] Pub. L. No. 112-96, § 6302(e)(1), 126 Stat. 156, 219.

[21] Pub. L. No. 112-96, § 6303(a), 126 Stat. 156, 221.

[22] The PSCR program also conducts research on behalf of the DHS Office for Interoperability and Compatibility in support of the development of public safety broadband.

[23] Pub. L. No. 112-96, § 6101, 126 Stat. 156, 205.

[24] Pub. L. No. 112-96, § 6201, 126 Stat. 156, 206.

[25] *In the Matter of Implementing Public Safety Broadband Provisions of the Middle Class Tax Relief and Job Creation Act of 2012; Implementing a Nationwide, Broadband, Interoperable Public Safety Network in the 700 MHz Band; Service Rules for the 698-746, 747-762 and 777-792 MHz Bands,* Second Report and Order, 28 FCC Rcd. 15174 (2013).

[26] Pub. L. No. 112-96, § 6402, 126 Stat. 156, 224.

[27] Pub. L. No. 112-96, § 6413(b)(3), 126 Stat. 156, 236. NTIA was allowed to borrow $2 billion from the U.S. Treasury to support FirstNet's work prior to the deposit of auction proceeds into the newly created Public Safety Trust Fund. NTIA must reimburse the Treasury from funds deposited into the Public Safety Trust Fund once the spectrum auctions are complete. Pub. L. No. 112-96, §§ 6207 and 6413(b), 126 Stat. 156, 215.

[28] Pub. L. No. 112-96, § 6208, 126 Stat. 156, 215.

[29] *In the Matter of Requests for Waiver of Various Petitioners to Allow the Establishment of 700 MHz Interoperable Public Safety Wireless Broadband Networks*, Order, 25 FCC Rcd 5145 (2010); *In the Matter of Requests for Waiver of Various Petitioners to Allow the Establishment of 700 MHz Interoperable Public Safety Wireless Broadband Networks*, Order, 26 FCC Rcd 6783 (2011).

[30] *Public Safety and Homeland Security Bureau Seeks Comment on Transition Process for 700 MHz Public Safety Broadband Waiver Recipients*, Public Notice, 27 FCC Rcd. 3310 (PSHSB 2012); *In the Matter of Implementing Public Safety Broadband Provisions of the Middle Class Tax Relief and Job Creation Act of 2012; Service Rules for the 698-746, 747-762 and 777-792 MHz Bands, Implementing a Nationwide, Broadband, Interoperable Public Safety Network in the 700 MHz Band,* Order, 27 FCC Rcd. 9652 (2012).

[31] NTIA was authorized to award BTOP grants through the American Recovery and Reinvestment Act of 2009, Pub. L. No. 111-5, 123 Stat. 115 (2009). Harris County, Texas, obtained a grant for its public-safety network project from the Federal Emergency Management Agency (FEMA), not BTOP.

[32] *In the Matter of Implementing Public Safety Broadband Provisions of the Middle Class Tax Relief and Job Creation Act of 2012; Service Rules for the 698-746, 747-762 and 777-792 MHz Bands, Implementing a Nationwide, Broadband, Interoperable Public Safety Network in the 700 MHz Band,* Order, 27 FCC Rcd. 9652 (2012).

[33] Universal Licensing System, License Call Sign WQQE234 (Nov. 15, 2012).

[34] According to FirstNet officials, various factors could affect whether the early builder networks are integrated into FirstNet's public safety network including whether a state "opts out" and builds its own RAN to connect to the FirstNet core, the desire of the state to retain the network and/or equipment, the individually negotiated infrastructure and maintenance agreements executed by the early builders with their vendors, if it is economically desirable or practical for FirstNet to utilize the network or equipment, and the ability to reach a timely and cost-effective agreement regarding the transfer or lease of network facilities.

[35] The Executive Office of the State of Mississippi was awarded a BTOP grant totaling $70.1 million to build its public-safety broadband network. The state used $32.1 million in BTOP funds, according to its last BTOP report submitted to NTIA. Negotiations for an SMLA failed due to disagreements between FirstNet and the state on a number of issues. Consequently, the Mississippi award expired. State officials told us that they were seeking information from NTIA on decommissioning the network, donating unused equipment to FirstNet, and continuing to use the microwave systems it deployed.

[36] A BTOP grant totaling $50.6 million was awarded to Motorola Solutions, Inc., the vendor selected to partner with the Bay Area Regional Interoperable Communications Systems, to build and operate a public safety network in the Bay Area. Motorola, Inc. reported in its last BTOP report to NTIA that it received $5.9 million in BTOP funds. Motorola, Inc. terminated the grant when it was unable to reach an SMLA with FirstNet.

[37] The City of Charlotte was awarded $16.7 million in BTOP funds to deploy a public-safety broadband network. Charlotte officials told us they repurposed the grant and planned to use the remaining $8.8 million of BTOP funds to improve the city's public-safety mobile technology and infrastructure.

[38] GAO-12-343.

[39] LTE has been accepted and adopted by national and international communities as the foundation for future mobile telecommunications.

[40] Pub. L. No. 112-96, § 6204(b), 126 Stat. 156, 209.

[41] Pub. L. No. 112-96, § 6205(a)(1), 126 Stat. 156, 211.

[42] FirstNet originally called this position "General Manager" but has since changed the position to "Executive Director." FirstNet's first Executive Director resigned in April 2014. As of February 2015, the position was still vacant and FirstNet's Deputy Executive Director is serving as Acting Executive Director.

[43] FirstNet's planned regional teams will mirror the 10 FEMA regions.

[44] For example, FirstNet is exploring whether it can use Temporary Appointments and Intergovernmental Personnel Act appointments, which allow for the temporary assignment of personnel between the federal government and state, local, and tribal governments; colleges and universities; federally funded research and development centers; and other organizations.

[45] The FAR is the comprehensive set of rules governing the process by which executive branch agencies purchase goods and services. Its purpose is to ensure purchasing procedures are standard and consistent, and conducted in a fair and impartial manner.

[46] 77 Fed. Reg. 60680 (Oct. 4, 2012).

[47] As such, this RFI also included a draft Statement of Objectives that interested parties were invited to comment on.

[48] Pub. L. No. 112-96, § 6206(d)(2), 126 Stat. 156, 215. The APA provides the basic framework of administrative law governing agency actions, including the procedural steps that must precede the effective promulgation, amendment, or repeal of a rule by a federal agency. Solicitation of comments on proposed legal interpretations and related items is typically performed through a Public Notice and comment process.

[49] 79 Fed. Reg. 57058 (Sept. 24, 2014).

[50] NPSTC is a federation of organizations whose mission is to improve public safety communications and interoperability through collaborative leadership.

[51] Pub. L. No. 112-96, § 6203(c)(1)(A), 126 Stat.156, 208. FCC Technical Advisory Board for First Responder Interoperability, *Recommended Minimum Technical Requirements to Ensure Nationwide Interoperability for the Nationwide Public Safety Broadband Network* (Washington, D.C.: May 22, 2012).

[52] "Priority" transmission of calls and data is provided through special enhancements embedded in telecommunications networks to identify transmissions made by authorized users as higher priority than those made by other users. These enhancements automatically place the transmission higher in the queue over those made by other users.

[53] NPSTC, *Defining Public Safety Grade Systems and Facilities* (Littleton, CO: May 22, 2014).

[54] Specifically, SPOCs responded this 33 percent of the time. For question wording, see appendix II question 5 (b-g).

[55] Specifically, 31 percent of SPOCs responded that they were "moderately satisfied" with FirstNet's progress carrying out a transparent RFI process; 31 percent responded that they were "moderately dissatisfied" with FirstNet's progress developing the technical and operational requirements of the network; and 27 percent responded that they were "moderately dissatisfied" with FirstNet's progress developing practices, procedures, and standards for managing and operating the network. For question wording, see appendix II question 5 (b-g).

[56] The PSAC established its Tribal Working Group in January 2015.

[57] Pub. L. No. 112-96, § 6302, 126 Stat. 156, 219.

[58] NTIA awarded these funds as part of SLIGP Phase I. SLIGP will have two phases; as of March 2015, Phase II has not commenced. NTIA, in consultation with FirstNet, will determine the timing of Phase II.

[59] For discussion of those core principles, see GAO, *Fisheries Management: Core Principles and a Strategic Approach Would Enhance Stakeholder Participation in Developing Quota-Based Programs*, GAO-06-289 (Washington, D.C.: Feb. 23, 2006). GAO-06-289 identified core principles for effective stakeholder participation by interviewing participation experts and reviewing academic literature on public participation theory and practice, policies from

leading federal agencies in stakeholder participation, and prior GAO work. See also, for example, GAO, *Aviation and the Environment: Systematically Addressing Environmental Impacts and Community Concerns Can Help Airports Reduce Project Delays*, GAO-10-50 (Washington, D.C.: Sept. 13, 2010).

[60] Twenty-two percent were "neither satisfied nor dissatisfied." These percentages do not equal 100 due to rounding and because one SPOC responded "do not know." For question wording, see appendix II question 15.

[61] Specifically, 54 percent of the time SPOCs responded "large increase" when asked how much more, if at all, FirstNet should focus on various items in its outreach to their states (such as design and construction of the core and radio access network, coverage areas, security requirements, training needs of users, and user fee pricing). For question wording, see appendix II question 13.

[62] GAO/AIMD-00-21.3.1; also see GAO-14-704G (effective Oct. 1, 2015).

[63] Due to the sensitive information about FirstNet's procurement activities contained in this roadmap, FirstNet has not publicly released the full version. The executive summary is available on FirstNet's website at http://www.firstnet.gov/content/march-board-directors-meeting.

[64] Due to the sensitive information about FirstNet's procurement and cost-estimating activities contained in this risk register, FirstNet has not publicly released it.

[65] I n addition to these formal periodic risk assessments, FirstNet officials also said in February 2015 that informal risk assessment is ongoing based on issues as identified and are handled as appropriate on a real-time basis.

[66] GAO, *Telecommunications: FCC Should Assess the Design of the E-rate Program's Internal Control Structure*, GAO-10-908 (Washington, D.C.: Sept. 29, 2010).

[67] As required by the 2012 act, an independent auditor audited FirstNet's financial statements as of September 2013, and FirstNet has submitted annual reports to Congress in each of the fiscal years since its creation. As of February 2015, NTIA was in the process of hiring a firm that will audit FirstNet's fiscal year 2014 and 2015 financial statements. Pub. L. No. 112-96, § 6209(a)(1), 126 Stat. 156, 216.

[68] Commerce OIG, *First Responder Network Authority: FirstNet Must Strengthen Management of Financial Disclosures and Monitoring of Contracts*, Final Report No. OIG-15-013-A (Washington, D.C.: Dec. 5, 2014).

[69] The Harris County, Texas, project has budgeted $500,000 per site for new sites as well.

[70] GAO-09-3SP.

[71] We did not analyze the quantitative input and output of the cost model because the data included procurement sensitive information, and we would therefore be unable to report our findings in a public report.

[72] As FirstNet develops its network and RFP, we may update our assessment of its cost estimate.

[73] Pub. L. No. 112-96, § 6206(c)(3), 126 Stat. 156, 214.

[74] Ryan Hallahan and John M. Peha, *The Business Case of a Network that Serves both Public Safety and Commercial Subscribers*, Telecommunications Policy, 35 (2011).

[75] This interoperable network in Sweden is called the "Rakel" network and is primarily used for voice communications.

[76] Pub. L. No. 112-96, § 6206(b)(2)(A), 126 Stat. 156, 212.

[77] FirstNet sought input into this matter in its September 2014 RFI.

[78] NPSTC, *Defining Public Safety Grade Systems and Facilities*, 2014.

[79] FCC, *A Broadband Network Cost Model: A Basis for Public Funding Essential to Bringing Nationwide Interoperable Communications to America's First Responders*, OBI Technical Paper No. 2 (May 2010).

[80] FirstNet sought input into this matter in its September 2014 RFI.

[81] Hallahan and Peha, 2011.

[82] According to FirstNet officials, these negative income flows could be borne by one or more commercial partners, depending on the public safety network construction and operation arrangements.

[83] More than 75 percent of survey respondents noted that the network would be "very useful" to emergency management, emergency medical services, fire services, and law enforcement. For question wording, see appendix II question 1.

[84] For question wording, see appendix II question 3.

[85] Additionally, about 84 percent of SPOCs we surveyed noted that FirstNet should largely or moderately increase its focus on user fee pricing in its outreach to their states. For question wording, see appendix II question 13.

[86] For question wording, see appendix II question 4.

[87] Additionally, the fees that FirstNet charges are subject to review by NTIA to ensure that they are sufficient to cover network costs.

[88] Pub. L. No. 112-96, § 6001(26), 126 Stat. 156, 204.

[89] FirstNet proposed some interpretations of these definitions in its September 2014 Public Notice. 79 Fed. Reg. 57058 (Sept. 24, 2014).

[90] One study showed that theoretically, the revenue to be derived from secondary use of the spectrum is much greater than fees from users of a public safety network. See Hallahan and Peha, 2011.

[91] Pub. L. No. 112-96, § 6208(a)(1), 126 Stat. 156, 215. FirstNet tentatively concluded in its September 2014 Public Notice that multiple commercial partners could coexist and utilize FirstNet spectrum in a given area. 79 Fed. Reg. 57058 (Sept. 24, 2014).

[92] This auction, for 65 MHz of spectrum, included 341 rounds of bidding. The auction resulted in over $40 billion in bids from over 30 bidders.

[93] According to FirstNet officials, the public safety network FirstNet is developing is more clearly defined than the network proposed in 2008 with the D Block. Further, FirstNet has been provided significant initial capital to establish this network, including the $7 billion from spectrum auctions and twice as much spectrum as the D Block.

[94] GAO-12-343.

[95] GAO-12-343.

[96] Mobile "deployables" can also be referred to as "deployable networks." A deployable network typically includes "deployable assets" such as "cells on wheels" that provide localized wireless network service to areas where coverage is minimal or compromised. These assets typically provide fully functional service via vehicles such as trailers, vans, and trucks.

[97] GAO-09-45. GAO-09-45 identified key features of an evaluation plan through the consultation of social science and evaluation literature, along with published GAO guidance.

[98] The plans identify the key-learning condition activities, including roles and responsibilities and the information, lessons, reports, and other deliverables expected under the SMLA.

[99] As one plan notes, the document "provides the requisite details on the required activities and each party's obligations, so that the learning conditions are effectively collected, documented, and applied to the nationwide public-safety network roll-out."

[100] FirstNet told us the consultants will be in position to obtain informal and formal "learnings." In this report, we will refer to these "learnings" as informal and formal lessons. An example of an informal lesson could come from the challenges experienced during a network build on various issues including the placement of antennas or the permit process, whereas a formal lesson could come from a key-learning condition specified in the SMLA.

[101] Pub. L. No 112-96, 126 Stat. 156.

[102] GAO, *Standards for Internal Control in the Federal Government*, GAO/AIMD-00-21.3.1 (Washington, D.C.: Nov. 1999). The most recent version of these standards was issued in September 2014. GAO, *Standards for Internal Control in the Federal Government*, GAO-14-704G (Washington, D.C.: Sept. 10, 2014).

[103] For discussion of those core principles, see GAO, *Fisheries Management: Core Principles and a Strategic Approach Would Enhance Stakeholder Participation in Developing Quota-*

Based Programs, GAO-06-289 (Washington, D.C.: Feb. 23, 2006). GAO-06-289 identified core principles for effective stakeholder participation by interviewing participation experts and reviewing academic literature on public participation theory and practice, policies from leading federal agencies in stakeholder participation, and prior GAO work.

[104] GAO, *GAO Cost Estimating and Assessment Guide: Best Practices for Developing and Managing Capital Program Costs*, GAO-09-3SP (Washington, D.C.: Mar. 2, 2009).

[105] We did not analyze the quantitative input and output of the cost model because the data included procurement sensitive information and we would therefore be unable to report our findings in a public report.

[106] FCC, *Technical Advisory Board for First Responder Interoperability, Recommended Minimum Technical Requirements to Ensure Nationwide Interoperability for the Nationwide Public Safety Broadband Network* (Washington, D.C.: May 22, 2012). NPSTC, *Defining Public Safety Grade Systems and Facilities* (Littleton, CO: May 22, 2014).

[107] GAO, *Tax Administration: IRS Needs to Strengthen Its Approach for Evaluating the SRFMI Data-Sharing Pilot Program*, GAO-09-45 (Washington, D.C.: Nov. 7, 2008). GAO-09-45 identified key features of an evaluation plan through the consultation of social science and evaluation literature, along with published GAO guidance.

[108] The 5 U.S. territories we surveyed were American Samoa, Guam, the Northern Mariana Islands, Puerto Rico, and the U.S. Virgin Islands.

[109] We conducted semi-structured interviews with all of these stakeholders and throughout this report we refer to “a few” of the stakeholders if officials from 3-5 entities, “some” if 6-9, “many” if 10-14, and “numerous” if 15 or more expressed the view.

In: The First Responder Network (FirstNet) ISBN: 978-1-63483-850-4
Editor: Margaret Saunders

Chapter 3

TESTIMONY OF SUSAN SWENSON, CHAIRWOMAN, FIRST RESPONDER NETWORK AUTHORITY (FIRSTNET). HEARING ON "THREE YEARS LATER: ARE WE ANY CLOSER TO A NATIONWIDE PUBLIC SAFETY WIRELESS BROADBAND NETWORK?"*

INTRODUCTION

Chairman Thune, Ranking Member Nelson and all Members of the Senate Commerce Committee, I would like to thank you for the opportunity to appear before the Committee to discuss FirstNet and the progress we are making toward the deployment of an interoperable nationwide public safety broadband network (network). I also want to thank all of the Members of this Committee who were pivotal in creating FirstNet. We look forward to your continued support and to working with the Committee as FirstNet continues to carry out our vital mission to bring the power of broadband wireless communications to public safety personnel across the country.

---

* This is an edited, reformatted and augmented version of testimony presented March 11, 2015 before the Senate Committee on Commerce, Science and Transportation.

Background

The Middle Class Tax Relief and Job Creation Act of 2012 (P.L. 112-96) (Act) established FirstNet as an independent authority within the Department of Commerce's National Telecommunications and Information Administration (NTIA). Under the Act, FirstNet is tasked with ensuring the deployment and operation of a sustainable, interoperable broadband network for public safety entities across the country and within U.S. territories. FirstNet intends to provide cutting-edge prioritized and preemptive wireless broadband communications to millions of first responders at the local, state, tribal, and Federal levels. Using a dedicated nationwide wireless broadband network, FirstNet will provide a ubiquitous solution to decades-long interoperability and communications challenges and help keep our communities and first responders safer with advanced communications services, devices, and applications.

FirstNet's goal of deploying the network to meet the needs of first responders is a matter of critical importance for public safety. While the task ahead will not be easy, FirstNet is developing the necessary leadership, staff, and support from states, tribes, public safety, and other key stakeholders to make this network a reality for first responders and the public who calls on them in its time of need.

Overarching Strategic Goals

To guide us, we are pursuing the following four strategic goals:

- Explore and build strong partnerships with local, state, tribal, and Federal jurisdictions;
- Establish a high-performaing organization and a culture of excellence;
- Ensure all resources are used efficiently to accomplish FirstNet's mission and demonstrate leadership towards self-sustainability to all external stakeholders; and
- Ensure the deployment and operation of a reliable, interoperable, and survivable nationwide Long Term Evolution (LTE) broadband network for public safety.

FirstNet is taking on an important and difficult task, but with the support of this Committee, Congress as a whole, the public safety community, the private sector, and local, state, tribal, and Federal leaders, we will succeed in accomplishing our mission. I would like to briefly discuss our recent accomplishments and describe where we are heading in an effort to support our nation's public safety personnel.

STRATEGIC ROADMAP AND FOUNDATIONAL NETWORK PLANNING

FirstNet is focused on what it will take from outreach, technical, and financial perspectives to build and maintain the network long-term. Much of our planning is embodied in FirstNet's Strategic Program Roadmap Executive Summary approved by the FirstNet Board in March 2014[1]. In that document, we outlined the milestones we planned to accomplish over the next year, which included:

- beginning formal in-person state consultations;
- releasing a draft request for comprehensive network proposals (RFP) for comment;
- releasing draft requests for certain network and equipment services proposals for comment; and
- initiating a public notice and comment process on certain program procedures, policies, and statutory interpretations.

FirstNet has made significant progress on these milestones. We:

- Distributed 56 state consultation packages on April 30, 2014. As of February 25, 2015, we have received 47 completed state checklists;
- Launched formal state consultations in July 2014 and have met with 15 states thus far, with an additional 24 scheduled through the summer;
- Published a Request for Information (RFI) with a draft Statement of Objectives for our comprehensive Request for Proposals (RFP) and received 122 comments; and

- Released a public notice seeking comment on several key program policies and statutory interpretations in the fall of 2014 and received 63 responses.

The progress we made in recent months is a tremendous start, but much work remains to be done. We will continue to work directly with the states and territories throughout our formal consultation process. Also, we will work to generate additional feedback from, local, state, and tribal public safety agencies, Federal stakeholders, the Public Safety Advisory Committee (PSAC), and the vendor community to ensure openness and transparency throughout our process.

CONSULTATION AND OUTREACH

Our efforts to interact with the local, state, tribal, and Federal stakeholders are a centerpiece of the FirstNet mission and are an essential requirement of the Act. Our local, state, and tribal planning consultation process, coordinated through the governor-designated state single points of contact (SPOCs), ensures that FirstNet obtains key information from the public safety community and leadership of all 56 states and territories. The objective of this process is to develop detailed state plans that address the unique communications needs of each state's public safety entities. These individual plans will inform and empower each state to choose to either have FirstNet deploy the radio access network (RAN) within its borders or to assume responsibility to build, operate and maintain its own state RAN and integrate it into the remainder of the nationwide network, as prescribed in the Act.

In order to execute on this statutory requirement, FirstNet has built a consultation strategy that focuses on several key objectives, ensuring that the consultation process is:

- iterative, giving states and other stakeholders opportunities to provide feedback and input in multiple ways and on an ongoing basis throughout;
- collaborative, so that we are working together with the localities, states, tribes, territories, and other stakeholders to collect information and data that will be useful for the deployment of the network;

- focused on critical elements, ensuring that we maximize the states' and taxpayers' investments in FirstNet; and
- informative to the development of FirstNet RFPs, the delivery of the state plans, and the design, construction, and operation of the network.

FirstNet anticipates holding in-person meetings with the 56 states and territories over the remainder of 2015 and beyond, and will continue to work closely with them as FirstNet moves into the phase of delivering wireless broadband service to their public safety personnel.

FirstNet held the first formal consultation meeting in July 2014 with leaders from the state of Maryland, including members from the Governor's office and executive agencies, the Maryland State Police, staff from the Maryland legislature, and other public safety leaders throughout the state. We learned valuable lessons about the state's emergency broadband communications needs, the state's perspective on the planning and deployment of the FirstNet network, and how we can build a strong partnership going forward.

Additionally, over the past year, FirstNet has conducted focused outreach with individual tribes, tribal associations, and Federal tribal government liaisons and worked with the PSAC to establish a Tribal Working Group. These discussions have resulted in positive dialogue and a better understanding of tribal needs. FirstNet hired a tribal outreach lead to assist with focused tribal outreach efforts, as well as a Federal Preservation Officer to address compliance with the National Historic Preservation Act.

While we are pleased with this progress in forging key partnerships through consultation, much more needs to be done. To that end, FirstNet is seeking to hire 10 regional teams to ensure sufficient resources in support of our outreach and state consultation efforts. These FirstNet regions cover the same state, territory, and tribal jurisdictions as the 10 Federal Emergency Management Agency (FEMA) regions. Our teams will span the nation to participate in state consultation meetings, join various regional and state governing body meetings and association conferences, and meet one-on-one with the SPOCs and public safety agencies representing potential FirstNet network users. FirstNet expects to hire these 10 regional leads in 2015.

Complementing this effort is FirstNet's robust outreach and education strategy, committed to reaching public safety personnel across all levels of government and through national and state associations. In the past year, we have addressed over 20,000 stakeholders at various conferences, meetings, and speaking events.

We are also working closely with Federal agencies to drive collaboration and potential use of the network. In 2014, FirstNet formalized a relationship with the Emergency Communications Preparedness Center (ECPC) to increase outreach with Federal stakeholders. The ECPC is the Federal interagency group focused on emergency communications, and is administered by the U.S. Department of Homeland Security's Office of Emergency Communications. FirstNet participated in many ECPC meetings over the past year to keep members informed of FirstNet activities and to discuss how best to collaborate to ensure Federal input is incorporated into the state plans and overall network deployment. Additionally, FirstNet's Federal outreach team held an initial formal consultation meeting with Federal agencies on January 21, 2015, where FirstNet staff engaged Federal stakeholders in discussions about outreach efforts, Federal coverage needs and objectives, and security requirements for the network. Finally, FirstNet has leveraged its Federal partners' expertise in the area of cybersecurity by utilizing recommendations and resources from the U.S. Department of Homeland Security's Office of Cybersecurity and Communications in our planning efforts.

Additionally, FirstNet's PSAC, chaired by Chief Harlin McEwen, and composed of key public safety stakeholders, will continue to be an important resource as we pursue our mission. Public safety's input via the PSAC is vital at all stages of the network development so that it will be tailored to the needs of the end users—America's first responders and other public safety entities.

The PSAC has to date collaboratively developed and delivered the following documents to FirstNet:

- Human Factors Report (November 2013): Analyzes the long-range impacts of the network on the way law enforcement, fire, and EMS operate and considers the impact the network will have on their duties once it is built and operating.[2]
- Potential Users – National Public Safety Broadband Network (NPSBN) (July 2014): Identifies and categorizes lists of potential network users.
- Use Cases for Interfaces, Applications, and Capabilities for the NPSBN (July 2014): Documents envisioned use cases for interfaces, applications, and capabilities for the network.

Issues that the PSAC is currently working on at FirstNet's request include the development of a proposed priority and preemption framework for the FirstNet network, and an analysis of the technical requirements of a broadband network dedicated to public safety entities.

We plan to continue to leverage the PSAC's experience to help inform key capabilities and functions of the network.

Organization and Leadership

In August 2012, the Secretary of Commerce fulfilled the statutory requirement of appointing the FirstNet Board. As required by law, the members have specialized knowledge, experience, and expertise from a variety of public safety, telecommunications, and financial backgrounds needed to develop the network. I was appointed as a Member of the Board at its inception, and I took over as Chairwoman in May 2014.

In September 2014, five new Board members joined the organization and we formally welcomed them during our September 2014 Board meeting. Those individuals are:

- Chris Burbank, Chief of Police, Salt Lake City Police Department;
- James H. Douglas, former Governor of Vermont;
- Annise Parker, Mayor, City of Houston, Texas;
- Frank Plastina, technology executive, North Carolina; and
- Richard Stanek, Sheriff, Hennepin County, Minnesota.

Along with the Board, FirstNet has hired key executives to guide the organization. TJ Kennedy has been serving as acting Executive Director and is responsible for day-to-day operations of the FirstNet organization. We have also built out our Chief Technology, Chief Financial, Chief Administrative, outreach, and legal teams during the past year, leveraging experience from both the private and public sectors.

Deployment and Operation of the Network

FirstNet also is actively conducting extensive market research to gain insight into the capabilities, opportunities, risks, and innovative business partnerships in the market today to support the construction of the network.

A. Requests for Information (RFI) and Draft Statement of Objectives (SOO)

From April 2013 through April 2014, FirstNet released 12 RFIs that focused on individual components of the network, including network partnering and RAN provisioning, antenna systems, microwave backhaul equipment, deployables, satellite service, enhanced packet core, transmission/transport, data centers, network management centers, network service platforms, devices, and applications. The results of these 12 RFIs, and the findings from numerous market research vendor meetings conducted by FirstNet, were compiled into an initial market research report that ultimately led to the development and release of the 13th RFI in September 2014. This RFI focused on soliciting feedback for a comprehensive network solution as opposed to individual network components and included a full draft SOO.

On September 17, 2014, the FirstNet Board authorized its release. The RFI sought input from industry on some of the key approaches FirstNet is considering before finalizing a draft comprehensive network RFP. The RFI included questions on network build out, deployment, operations, and maintenance; cost considerations and financial sustainability; speed to market; system hardening and resiliency; user priority and preemption; customer care and marketing; and general compliance with the Act.

The draft SOO has helped industry better understand FirstNet's key program objectives to deploy, operate, and maintain the network. FirstNet is taking an objectives-based approach to the procurement, rather than a requirements-driven approach, in order to promote flexibility in achieving our goals while helping us reduce the complexity we face in managing and integrating the diverse set of components needed to meet our mission. FirstNet will use the comments we receive on the RFI and draft SOO to refine the acquisition approach and draft the comprehensive network RFP.

As previously referenced, we received 122 responses to this RFI and were very encouraged with the interest it generated. All responses have been kept confidential to allow the RFI respondents to provide comprehensive and forthright solutions, facilitating FirstNet's ability to thoroughly develop the next step in the procurement phase – the drafting of the RFP. It is important to note that the responses came not only from the vendor community, but also from several state, local, and public safety entities. We take this as another positive sign that the public safety community is highly engaged and supportive of our mission.

FirstNet is statutorily required to engage in an open, transparent, and competitive RFP process, and the publication of this latest RFI is an important step in meeting this obligation. This RFI/draft SOO continues FirstNet's market research efforts and acts as a precursor to the publication of a draft RFP and a final RFP anticipated to be released by early 2016.

B. Public Notice and Comment

In September 2014, FirstNet also received Board approval to seek public comment on its statutory interpretations. As a new entity operating under a unique statutory construct, FirstNet is confronted with many complex legal issues and terms that will have a material impact on our RFPs and our operations going forward. Although FirstNet is exempt from the procedural requirements of the Administrative Procedure Act (APA), we believe it is important to solicit public comments on certain technical, economic, and foundational legal issues to inform our approach to our ongoing operations and to further consult with our stakeholders. Specifically, we sought comments on issues that included the interpretation of the definitions of core and RAN; the definition of public safety entities; secondary users; rural areas; user and other fees; and finally, the minimum technical requirements of the network.

We received more than 60 responses to this public notice and have continued to review and digest the information provided in each response. We received responses from a broad group of stakeholders, including commercial carriers, vendors, state, local, and tribal governments, and various associations that represent public safety interests.

On March 9, 2015, the FirstNet Board approved the release of a second public notice seeking comments on management's additional preliminary interpretations of FirstNet's enabling legislation. The primary topics covered include technical requirements relating to equipment and device use on the network, the nature and application of required network policies, FirstNet's presentation of state plans, and the rights and responsibilities of states choosing to build and operate their own RANs.

We believe public comments on these topics will provide important inputs into a draft comprehensive network RFP and on FirstNet operations, including on issues that will significantly impact the economics of the network. The public notice will also inform our stakeholders of our preliminary thinking on critical decisions relating to the deployment and operation of the network. The responses to this notice will be made part of the public record and be available at www.regulations.gov for public review.

C. Additional Technical Development and PSCR Collaboration

In addition to leading the analysis of the industry and public responses to the comprehensive network RFI, which will inform a comprehensive draft RFP, the FirstNet technical team has been focusing on a number of core areas:

- Formal standards development;
- Testing and evaluation; and
- Modeling and simulation.

We have been working very closely with the Department of Commerce's team at the Public Safety Communications Research (PSCR) labs to share ideas and data and to eliminate information silos. Working directly with PSCR has allowed FirstNet to make significant progress with the Third Generation Partnership Project (3GPP), the worldwide standards body for LTE, on ways in which LTE standards can meet public safety's unique needs.[3] As a result of this collaboration, FirstNet has helped to develop broad coalitions that have pushed for the prioritization of public safety standards development in worldwide LTE standards.

In addition, the FirstNet technical team has assisted in validating certain key assumptions within the FirstNet Strategic Program Roadmap Summary, including the modeling of cell site location nationwide and the amount of excess network capacity that might be available for secondary use.

FirstNet will continue to work with PSCR throughout the development of the network. We have already seen tremendous benefit from our cooperative relationship and we look forward to continuing this productive collaboration.

Early Builder Public Safety Projects

FirstNet has executed five spectrum manager lease agreements (SMLAs), with Adams County in Colorado,[4] the State of New Jersey,[5] the State of New Mexico, the Los Angeles Regional Interoperable Communications System Authority (LA-RICS), and the State of Texas (allowing for public safety broadband network service in Harris County). As a result of these agreements, FirstNet now is working closely with five early builder projects to gather lessons that will help drive efficiencies and better understanding of key factors important to the design and development of the network.[6]

Each of these projects is detailed in depth in the attached FY 2014 Annual Report to Congress, attached to this testimony for your reference.

CULTURE OF COMPLIANCE

Over the past year, FirstNet has grown significantly in our organizational structure, and this growth has provided greater resources, rigor, and oversight in the management of our operations. By hiring senior managers and staff during FY 2014, FirstNet has implemented policies and procedures that provide clear direction and structure for the organization. Our FY 2014 Annual Report to Congress goes into detail on the steps that we have taken to strengthen our compliance processes.[7]

FirstNet has also incorporated lessons learned from an Inspector General (OIG) report examining certain processes relating to Board member financial disclosure filings and identification of potential conflicts of interest and procurement oversight practices.[8]

FirstNet has a positive working relationship with the OIG, and we look forward to continuing our open and constructive coordination with this office.

CONCLUSION

I am grateful to the Committee for the opportunity to update you on FirstNet's progress. As you can see, FirstNet continues its efforts to meet statutory obligations, partner with those who will use and benefit from the network, and develop a business plan that will provide innovative broadband services to public safety personnel on a long-term, self-funded basis.

FirstNet is committed to achieving our objectives, but we can only do so with the support of Congress, public safety, locals, states, tribal jurisdictions, and our other stakeholders. This is a network that is urgently needed to increase the safety and capabilities of all public safety personnel and protect the American people, and we are committed to delivering it.

End Notes

[1] The FirstNet Strategic Program Roadmap Executive Summary can be accessed at: http://firstnet.gov/content/march-board-directors-meeting.

[2] The FirstNet PSAC Human Factors Report, available at: http://www.firstnet.gov/sites/default/files/PSAC%20Human%20Factors%20Report-FINAL.pdf.

[3] The standards body through which we are working is The 3rd Generation Partnership Project (3GPP). According to the 3GPP website, "3GPP unites [six] telecommunications standard development organizations (ARIB, ATIS, CCSA, ETSI, TTA, TTC) and provides a stable environment to produce the Reports and Specifications that define 3GPP technologies." 3GPP website, "About 3GPP." available at: http://www.3gpp.org/about-3gpp/about-3gpp.

[4] Adams County Communications Center, Inc.

[5] State of New Jersey Office of Information Technology.

[6] Four of these projects are funded through NTIA's Broadband Technology Opportunities Program (BTOP) grants that were awarded prior to passage of the Act. The Harris County project was funded through a pre-Act Department of Homeland Security grant.

[7]. N/A.

[8] On December 5, 2014, the Department of Commerce's OIG released a report entitled "FirstNet Must Strengthen Management of Financial Disclosures and Monitoring of Contracts." Available at: http://www.oig.doc.gov/Pages/FirstNet-Must-Strengthen-Management-of-Financial-Disclosures-and-Monitoringof-Contracts.aspx.

In: The First Responder Network (FirstNet) ISBN: 978-1-63483-850-4
Editor: Margaret Saunders

Chapter 4

TESTIMONY OF TODD J. ZINSER, INSPECTOR GENERAL, U.S. DEPARTMENT OF COMMERCE. HEARING ON "THREE YEARS LATER: ARE WE ANY CLOSER TO A NATIONWIDE PUBLIC SAFETY WIRELESS BROADBAND NETWORK?"*

Chairman Thune, Ranking Member Nelson, and Members of the Committee:

We appreciate the opportunity to testify about the current status of and challenges encountered by the First Responder Network Authority (FirstNet). Effective oversight of FirstNet is critical. Our last three *Top Management Challenges* (*TMC*) reports, for fiscal years (FY) 2013 through 2015, included addressing First Net's implementation of a nationwide wireless broadband network for public safety users among the most significant management and performance challenges facing the Department of Commerce.

Our testimony today, about 3 years after the passage of the Middle Class Tax Relief and Job Creation Act of 2012[1] that established FirstNet, will focus on (I) FirstNet's work to date; (II) the Office of Inspector General's (OIG's) completed oversight efforts; (III) OIG's ongoing oversight of FirstNet; and (IV) the continuing challenges the Department and FirstNet face in their

* This is an edited, reformatted and augmented version of testimony presented March 11, 2015 before the Senate Committee on Commerce, Science and Transportation.

efforts to ensure implementation of a nationwide, interoperable, wireless broadband network for the public safety community.

I. Introduction to FirstNet

Establishment and purpose

Signed into law on February 22, 2012, the Middle Class Tax Relief and Job Creation Act of 2012 (the Act) established FirstNet as an independent authority within the Department of Commerce's National Telecommunications and Information Administration (NTIA). The Act authorized and allocated up to $7 billion in funding to NTIA for the establishment of an interoperable Nationwide Public Safety Broadband Network (NPSBN). This network is being built to address failures that occurred in the United States on September 11, 2001, during the terrorist attacks, in which first responders could not effectively communicate.

FirstNet is governed by a 15-member Board consisting of the Attorney General of the United States, the Secretary of Homeland Security, the Director of the Office of Management and Budget, and 12 nonpermanent members, including representatives from state and local governments the public safety community, and technical fields. After a public recruitment process, NTIA recommended candidates to the Acting Secretary of Commerce, who announced the appointments in August 2012. The Board's first meeting was held in September 2012. The Act calls for the termination of FirstNet 15 years after its enactment, in 2027.[2] However, no later than 10 years after the Act's enactment, in 2022, the Comptroller General of the United States must submit to Congress a report on what action Congress should take regarding this 2027 sunset provision.[3]

Organization and Initial Implementation

For roughly the first year and a half of its existence, certain FirstNet Board members functioned in management roles. The Board eventually assembled a management team which assumed all operational responsibilities (see section IV for further details). As of December 2014, FirstNet is organized with multiple program offices reporting to a Deputy Executive Director along with divisions covering areas such as procurement, user advocacy, financial operations, legal counsel, information technology and administration.

So far, implementation of the NPSBN has occurred in the following areas:

- *Establishing an organizational structure.* FirstNet hired key leadership and support staff for its day-to-day operations; developed internal controls; established its headquarters in Reston, Virginia, and its technical headquarters in Boulder, Colorado; awarded contracts to obtain project management and planning support, professional and subject matter support, and network and business plan development; and signed interagency agreements with other federal entities to provide key services.
- *Conducting initial consultation and outreach.* FirstNet launched a website, conducted conference calls and webinars with state single points of contact, coordinated with NTIA's State and Local Implementation Grant Program (SLIGP) team, and established its Public Safety Advisory Committee (PSAC).[4] In July 2014, FirstNet began to hold a series of state consultation meetings. As of March 2, 2015, 15 of these state consultations had been held.
- *Finalizing a network design approach.* In FY 2013, FirstNet issued 12 requests for information (RFIs) seeking input from vendors and other stakeholders; in FY 2014, it issued another RFI—for assistance in developing a comprehensive network acquisition strategy—and issued a public notice and request for comments seeking input regarding preliminary interpretations of FirstNet's enabling legislation. It also established spectrum lease agreements with four public-safety projects funded by NTIA's Broadband Technology Opportunities Program (BTOP) grant awards program.

FirstNet's current focus is on the consultation and the acquisition/request for proposal (RFP) processes.

Funding and Expenditures

The Act authorizes up to $7 billion in funding to FirstNet for deployment of the NPSBN. Initial funding of FirstNet will come from Federal Communications Commission (FCC) spectrum auction proceeds. The FCC spectrum auction, completed in January 2015, raised about $45 billon, enough to cover the $7 billion targeted for FirstNet under the Act. FirstNet holds the single Public Safety Wireless Network License for use of the 700 MHz D block spectrum and a pre-existing block of public safety broadband spectrum.

Over the long term, FirstNet must be self-sustaining, through user fees and revenue generated from agreements with third parties that will leverage the value of the network capacity.

FirstNet's expenditures are expected to increase as it moves toward building the NPSBN. FirstNet reported that it spent less than $250,000 in FY 2012. In FY 2013, it spent about $17 million, and in FY 2014, it spent an estimated $26 million.[5] In September 2014, FirstNet's Board approved a budget of $120 million for FY 2015. Its FY 2016 budget proposal is for approximately $160 million. This will provide funding for approximately 150 full-time-equivalent positions, as well as additional contracting and administrative support. FirstNet has entered into various interagency agreements, hired support contractors and, in September 2013, issued a $67.2 million blanket purchase agreement (BPA) with three contractors for technical and subject matter expert support tasks, to be issued over a 2- year period.

II. OIG's FirstNet Oversight to Date

FirstNet's authorizing legislation did not contain a direct provision for permanent, ongoing oversight. The law provides for two required reviews: (1) an annual independent audit of FirstNet's financial operations and condition and (2) a Government Accountability Office (GAO) report, not later than 10 years after enactment of the Act, or in the year 2022, on what action Congress should take regarding FirstNet's 15-year sunset provision. Nonetheless, since FirstNet is part of the Department of Commerce, and given the importance of this program and substantial commitment of public funds, our office is exercising oversight.

We have established a dedicated audit and evaluations team to oversee the Department's and FirstNet's effort. In addition, we operate a fraud, waste, and abuse hotline for the Department of Commerce through which we have received complaints related to FirstNet and we conduct follow-up on those complaints.

Building on OIG's experience with broadband and public safety programs (e.g., the Public Safety Interoperable Communications grant program and BTOP), the team's initial audit and evaluation activities have included:

- Tracking the progress of FirstNet by observing Board proceedings, meeting with NTIA and FirstNet officials, monitoring FirstNet and NTIA for key actions taken to implement the network, and reviewing key program documents (e.g., *Federal Register* notices and webinar slide decks)
- Developing an initial risk assessment in FY 2013 and reassessing risk as part of annual Department-wide assessments
- Identifying FirstNet as a management challenge in our FYs 2013–2015 *Top Management Challenges* reports
- Providing an information memorandum for FirstNet in February 2014 to identify FirstNet's initial management challenges (including establishing an effective organization, fostering cooperation among various state and local public safety agencies, integrating existing grants to enhance public communications capabilities into FirstNet, and creating a nationwide long-term evolution network)

In addition, we issued a December 2014 audit report on ethics- and procurement-related issues raised by a FirstNet Board member in 2013.[6] At an April 23, 2013, FirstNet Board of Directors meeting, a Board member presented a resolution raising various concerns, including (1) openness and transparency in decision making by the FirstNet Board, (2) Board members access to records, (3) the development of a plan for FirstNet's NPSBN, and (4) issues related to ethics and procurement. In addition, the Board member met with the Inspector General in July 2013 to discuss his concerns.

In May 2013, the FirstNet Board established a Special Review Committee to examine these issues. In the public version of its report,[7] the Committee concluded that (1) the FirstNet Board had engaged in open and transparent decision making, (2) FirstNet did not withhold information from Board members, and (3) FirstNet was still developing its network plan with full consultation and outreach. In October 2013, the Board chairman, based on conversations with the Inspector General, asked the OIG to take over the inquiry into ethics and procurement.

Our audit work, which covered 2012 and 2013, found:

A. *Confidential and public disclosure monitoring procedures were inadequate, some Board members did not file timely disclosure reports, and monitoring of potential conflicts of interest needs improvement.* Because of their status as special government employees and their level of compensation, FirstNet Board members are required to file confidential or public financial disclosure reports. The Department's Office of General Counsel (OGC) provided guidance to FirstNet Board members, each of whom was required to submit the confidential financial disclosure form; OGC also informed us that it initially provided ethics briefings for Board members, with counselling for those whose employment or financial interests could have created a conflict of interest.

The Department did not consider that some FirstNet Board members would devote enough time to their Board duties to trigger the requirement for the public financial disclosure form. Eight Board members did trigger the requirement in 2013.

Specifically, we found that OGC was unable to provide a record of all FirstNet confidential and public financial disclosure files, including due dates, as required by federal regulations. Nor had OGC created a schedule of Board members' start dates of service, due dates of disclosures, or a centralized point of record showing the training and counselling provided. In addition, 6 months after the Board began regular meetings, senior NTIA and OGC officials were still debating how best to routinely monitor potential conflicts of interest.

One Board member initially did not file a required public disclosure and, when eventually doing so, did not disclose an interest in a conflicting company. Another Board member submitted the required public disclosure form 5 months late. Two others submitted inaccurate time-and-attendance records, in one case to avoid filing the required public financial disclosure. Finally, all four of these Board members continued to engage in decision making, even though they were not in compliance with the financial disclosure requirements.

Our report included a Department response stating that—although certain administrative requirements may not have been fulfilled with respect to disclosure—as far as the Department is aware, Board members made the material disclosures necessary to identify and address potential conflicts. The Department also stated that OIG did not identify any violations of conflict of interest laws or circumstances that actually affected decision making. In its February 3, 2015 action plan and March 5, 2015 revision to the plan requested by our office, the Department identified actions taken to address these findings. In this response, the Department asserts that various matters related to financial disclosures have been addressed. FirstNet has developed compliance procedures and now coordinates with the Department on financial disclosures and conflicts of interest.

B. FirstNet's contracting practices lacked transparent award competition, sufficient oversight of hiring, and adequate monitoring. NTIA was tasked with helping FirstNet with its start-up efforts, including the procurement of professional staffing services such as project management and planning support, professional and intellectual support, and support to develop network and business plans. Because NTIA does not have a contracting office, it secured contracting assistance from other Departmental bureaus. Between September 2012 and March 2013, the contracting offices at the Census Bureau and the National Institute of Standards and Technology (NIST) entered into three timeand-material (T&M) contracts on behalf of NTIA to meet FirstNet's procurement needs.

T&M/labor hour contracts are considered high risk because a contractor's profit is tied to the number of hours worked; therefore, the government assumes the risk for cost overruns. Because of this risk, OMB's Office of Federal Procurement Policy (OFPP)[8] requires agencies to provide appropriate government monitoring of contractor performance to give reasonable assurance that efficient methods and effective cost controls are being used.

We found that the three contracts were awarded as T&M contracts, with a total value of approximately $14 million (see table 1, next page). Although contract 1 was properly awarded and administered, contracts 2 and 3 were not, as a result of the following:

- Sole-source procurement for contract 3 did not meet Federal Acquisition Regulation (FAR) exceptions to full and open competition requirements. The FAR—with limited exceptions—requires government agencies to procure services by obtaining full and open competition through procedures such as soliciting sealed bids and requesting competitive proposals. There are exceptions to obtaining full and open competition when one of several circumstances exists: for example, when (1) there is an unusual and compelling urgency or (2) the procurement is authorized or required by a statute expressly authorizing or requiring an acquisition from a specified source or through another agency. Our review of the justification for the sole source award of the third contract—which NIST awarded noncompetitively to Workforce Resources, Inc. (WRI) for \$8.40 million on March 18, 2013—showed that the justification was inadequate.

According to NIST, it awarded contract 3 noncompetitively because it was the most expeditious way to meet the Act's requirement to establish FirstNet as operational within certain deadlines. Additionally, the contracting office stated in its Justification for Other Than Full and Open Competition (JOFOC) that the procurement was unusual, urgent, and compelling—and that the interruption in services would be costly, as FirstNet had mission essential milestone dates that had to be executed to meet criteria established under the Act. We determined that the justification was inadequate because (a) we found that neither the Act nor the JOFOC identified specific guidelines FirstNet was required to meet and (b) procurement needs did not meet criteria for unusual and compelling urgency.

- Undue influence from a FirstNet official, which interfered with the contractor's ability to independently recruit and hire consultants. On two separate contracts, a FirstNet Board member inappropriately directed WRI hiring actions. First, before contract 2 was awarded, the government inappropriately identified and recruited subject matter experts (SMEs). Specifically, FirstNet directed WRI via NIST's contracting office to include a total of 16 SMEs in its proposal. On November 6, 2012—9 days prior to contract award (i.e., November 15, 2012)—NIST e-mailed WRI a spreadsheet containing the names of 14 SMEs. In addition, NIST also confirmed that 12 of the 16 SMEs included in the proposal were recommended directly by a FirstNet Board member, while the other 4 SMEs were transitioned in from the previous engagement with FunctionalIT (contract 1). The actions taken by the government gave the appearance that, in order to be awarded the contract, WRI was required to hire the SMEs recommended by the government.

  Neither contracts 2 nor 3 were designated as personal services contracts; however, in both cases, FirstNet directed the hiring of preselected SMEs. Control over hiring and firing decisions is one aspect of the traditional employer-employee relationship, and thus the exercise of such control by federal employees over contractor personnel can create the appearance of a personal service contracts. Federal agencies generally may not enter into such contracts without explicit authority to do so, essentially because they circumvent the civil service system. In response to our report, FirstNet did not assert that it has this authority. Furthermore, NIST and NTIA contracting personnel should have implemented stronger controls to ensure an independent relationship with contractor personnel—by both allowing the contractor to independently conduct SME recruitment and by not allowing FirstNet to direct hiring actions. Unduly close personal relationships with contractor personnel can create the appearance of favoritism and may call into question the integrity of the procurement process.

- Adequate surveillance not being conducted over contracts 2 and 3, resulting in approximately $11 million in unsupported costs to the government. Contracts 2 and 3, which were T&M contracts, required a level of monitoring that FirstNet ultimately did not provide. Although the Contracting Officer's Representative (COR) appropriately and consistently rejected incorrect invoices, the COR was also required to review all draft and final work products for "completeness, accuracy, and appropriateness." However, we were unable to verify that this monitoring actually occurred. We also could not conclude that—at the end of both contract periods—FirstNet received the few deliverables that were expressly required by the contracts (i.e., monthly status reports). WRI acknowledged that NIST did not require it to provide monthly status reports of tasks performed, even though such reports were required in contract 3.

Table 1. Summary of FirstNet's Time-and-Materials (T&M) Contracts in FY 2012 and 2013

Contracting Bureau (and Contract Number)	Date	Contractor	Contract Value (Millions)
Census Bureau (Contract 1)	09/13/2012	FunctionalIT	$1.95
NIST (Contract 2)	11/15/2012	Workforce Resources, Inc.	$3.98
NIST (Contract 3)	03/18/2013	Workforce Resources, Inc.	$8.40
Total			$14.33

Source: OIG analysis of FirstNet reports.

Note: Contract 1 was awarded to FunctionalIT for $1.95 million on September 13, 2012, with a performance period ending on March 21, 2014. Contract 2 was awarded to Workforce Resources, Inc. (WRI) for $3.98 million on November 15, 2012, and was terminated on March 17, 2013, after $2.59 million was expended. Contract 3 was also awarded to WRI for $8.4 million on March 18, 2013, with a performance period ending on December 17, 2013.

In its response to our report, the Department stated that it monitored the performance of its early contracts and that it relied on an unusual and compelling urgency exception to full and open competition. The Department also concurred with our recommendations related to the procurement issues noted in our report. In its February 3, 2015, action plan and March 5, 2015, revision to the plan requested by our office, the Department identified actions planned and taken to address these findings, including its plan to provide guidance to contracting staff on correct procedures for (1) selecting contract types, (2) hiring consultants, (3) ensuring receipt of deliverables, and (4) outreach, training, and oversight effort to prevent occurrences of unauthorized commitments. We are currently reviewing the revised plan.

III. CURRENT AUDIT WORK

OIG continues its oversight of FirstNet. In November 2014, OIG initiated an audit of FirstNet's technical development of the NPSBN. We initiated our audit after coordinating with the GAO, which had already started an ongoing review.[9] Our objectives are to evaluate and assess FirstNet's efforts and progress to develop the technical design aspects for the NPSBN against key technical requirements and standards, the requirements of the Act, stakeholder requirements, and established performance metrics and milestones. These activities are central to FirstNet achieving its mission to ensure the creation, deployment, and operation of a single, nationwide network design of the NPSBN. We plan to issue a final report on our audit later in FY 2015.

We are currently reviewing interagency agreements used to support FirstNet operations along with its work with entities such as PSAC, NIST, and the FCC to determine whether FirstNet fulfilled consultation requirements of the Act. It is important for FirstNet to consult and collaborate with these entities—which, having expertise regarding interoperable communications networks and knowledge of public safety needs, can provide significant input to how the network can be designed successfully. We are also reviewing expenditures and costs related to technical design efforts to assess spending levels, and information related to initial state consultation meetings to assess progress in incorporating key state concerns into the development of the technical design.

Establishing the NPSBN requires coordination and buy-in from regional, state, tribal, and local jurisdictions. As designated by the Act, FirstNet began consultation with Single Points of Contact (SPOCs) from each state that were established to represent the needs of the different jurisdictions. In April 2014, FirstNet began a process to meet with each state to understand their unique communication needs for the network and to allow an exchange of ideas and questions about the NPSBN. As part of this process, the SPOCs invite members of the public safety community to attend the consultation meetings. FirstNet identified that the initial consultation meetings will be an important step to an iterative, ongoing state consultation process. To date, FirstNet has completed some consultations and has scheduled others through the end of FY 2015. However, as of March 2, 2015, FirstNet had not scheduled all initial state consultations.

In February 2015, we attended FirstNet's initial state consultation effort with the state of Delaware—an event attended by the SPOC and other public safety officials throughout the state. The purpose of our visit was to assess FirstNet's approach to meeting its state consultation requirements. We are considering how FirstNet provides updates on its efforts to develop the NPSBN, as well as how it acquires information from public safety attendees and their unique first responder needs. Our review of a sample of FirstNet state consultation meetings with local first responders found that their key concerns were the cost of participation in the NPSBN; the necessity of priority status for first responders and the ability to preempt other users when accessing a network; and FirstNet's ability to facilitate rural coverage. In addition, some meeting participants called attention to issues unique to their states, for example rugged terrain or reoccurring catastrophic weather events such as hurricanes or tornadoes.

IV. Continuing Challenges for the Department and FirstNet

Three years after the passage of the Act, FirstNet faces various short- and long-term challenges. As it proceeds, the Department and FirstNet will require continued oversight from OIG, GAO, and Congress. Among the most significant challenges are:

- Ensuring the adequacy of funding for a nationwide network
- Determining the sufficiency of assets contributed to the network by states, local governments and commercial entities

- Incorporating lessons learned from the Broadband Technology Opportunities Program (BTOP)
- Addressing identified internal control weaknesses
- Addressing staffing and other organizational issues
- Effectively executing the consultation process

Adequacy of Funding for a Nationwide Long-Term Evolution (LTE) Network

The Act provides up to $7 billion to build a nationwide public safety network. FirstNet must build a network that covers most of the 50 states, 5 territories, the District of Columbia, and 556 tribal nations. The 3.8 million square miles to be covered by the network will include areas that are urban, suburban, rural, and wilderness, as well as islands. Although up to $7 billion was initially authorized by the Act, the total costs to establish the network are still unknown.

Sufficiency of Assets Contributed to the Network

Implementing the NPSBN will require that FirstNet leverage existing infrastructure, such as existing government and commercial buildings, towers, fiber or microwave backhaul, and data centers. Assets are expected to be contributed by various parties, including states, local governments, tribal entities, and commercial entities. FirstNet must effectively identify which existing infrastructure assets can be incorporated into the network. Also, FirstNet must take appropriate steps to comply with all applicable environmental and historic preservation laws, regulations, treaties, conventions, agreements, and executive orders as it integrates contributed assets into its design.

Lessons Learned

FirstNet will need to build upon lessons learned from public safety projects funded by BTOP grants, an American Recovery and Reinvestment Act of 2009 program administered by NTIA to expand nationwide broadband infrastructure and adoption. Of the approximately 230 BTOP awards, 7 went to establish regional public safety broadband networks. However, the passage of legislation establishing FirstNet overtook these projects, and all 7 BTOP awards were partially suspended. Eventually, FirstNet entered into spectrum lease agreements with 4 of the projects. These included grants made to Adams County Communications Center, Inc., Colorado; the Los Angeles Regional Interoperable Communications System Authority; the New Jersey Department of Treasury; and the New Mexico Department of Information Technology. For these ongoing projects, FirstNet will provide technical support and will share any lessons learned on issues such as quality of service, priority/pre-emption, and federal partnerships with the broader public safety community. FirstNet also needs to work closely with the Department of Commerce's Public Safety Communications Research (PSCR) program, which provides support in broadband technologies evaluation and testing, network modeling and simulation, and standards.

Previously Identified Internal Control Weaknesses

Initially, FirstNet struggled to establish an organization and necessary internal controls. In July 2014, an independent public accounting firm[10] reported a material weakness related to the financial reporting process in FirstNet's first financial statement audit required under the Act.

Additionally, as mentioned previously in this testimony, our December 2014 report on ethics- and procurement-related issues found that the Department's monitoring procedures for financial disclosure and potential conflicts of interest at FirstNet were inadequate. We also found that FirstNet's contracting practices lacked transparent award competition, sufficient oversight of hiring, and adequate monitoring. As we previously noted, the Department has acknowledged OIG's findings, concurred with our recommendations, and is undertaking corrective actions.

Staffing and Other Organizational Issues

FirstNet has encountered difficulties in hiring and maintaining staff for key technical positions. Nevertheless, FirstNet has made progress in establishing a management structure. For instance, certain Board members no longer play dual roles as Board members and managers. As noted above, for roughly the first year and a half of its existence, certain Board members functioned in roles as both board members and as part of the management team, before FirstNet eventually assembled a separate management team and transferred operational responsibilities to it. Nonetheless, while many senior positions (e.g., chief information officer, chief administrative officer, chief counsel, and chief financial officer) are in place, key leadership positions throughout the organization remain vacant, including the chief user advocacy officer—a leadership position managing consultation and outreach—as well as regional directors and supervisors for consultations. Two FirstNet executives have left their positions, which are now being filled in an acting capacity.

Effective Execution of the Consultation Process

The Act designates at least three federal agencies—the FCC, NTIA, and NIST—to provide consultation and support to FirstNet. The Act also required the creation of the PSAC to assist FirstNet in meeting its mission.

The Act also directed that FirstNet consult with regional, state, tribal and local jurisdictions regarding the distribution and expenditure of funds required to establish network policies. Cooperation from these jurisdictions is a significant factor in ensuring the successful deployment and sustainability of the NPSBN. Specific consultation topics outlined in the Act include core network construction and Radio Access Network (RAN) build out, placement of towers, and network coverage areas, among others.

FirstNet is to consult with the jurisdictions through a locally designated officer or body, generally referred to as the Single Point of Contact (SPOC) for each jurisdiction. Accordingly, FirstNet has begun initial consultations with SPOCs and must consider the information it collects into the NPSBN's development. FirstNet had set an internal goal to have initial consultations with each jurisdiction completed by the end of November 2014. However, while FirstNet has held some initial consultation meetings and has scheduled others into September 2015, many have yet to be scheduled (see table 2, next page). FirstNet has indicated that the timing of these meetings depends on each state's readiness and how quickly FirstNet can fully staff its outreach team.

Table 2. Status of First Net's Initial State and Local Consultation Meetings as of March 2, 2015

Status	Number
Completed	15
Scheduled	26
Not scheduled	15
Total	56

Source: OIG, based on FirstNet data.

Note: The target date for completion of meetings is November 30, 2014.

As we continue our oversight of FirstNet, we will keep the committee informed of FirstNet's progress with respect to the challenges discussed here—and any others we identify through our audits and investigations.

End Notes

[1] Middle Class Tax Relief and Job Creation Act of 2012, Pub. L. No. 112-96.

[2] Id. § 6206(f).

[3] Id. § 6206(g).

[4] The Middle Class Tax Relief and Job Creation Act of 2012 required FirstNet to establish the PSAC. It was created in February 2013 and consists of 40 members representing all disciplines of public safety as well as state, territorial, tribal, and local governments. See "Public Safety Advisory Committee" www.firstnet.gov/about/publicsafety-advisory-committee.

[5] Outlays, not expenses, were provided for FY 2012. FirstNet began financial reporting in FY 2013. The FY 2014 results have not been audited yet.

[6] U.S. Department of Commerce Office of Inspector General, December 5, 2014. FirstNet Must Strengthen Management of Financial Disclosures and Monitoring of Contracts, OIG-15-013-A. Washington, DC: DOC OIG. See this report for additional detail.

[7] See FirstNet Special Review Committee, September 20, 2013. Report on Openness and Transparency, Access to Information and Network Planning [online]. www.ntia.doc.gov/other-publication/2013/firstnet-special-reviewcommittee-report.

[8] OFPP memorandum, October 27, 2009. "Increasing Competition and Structuring Contracts for the Best Results."

[9] The GAO review assesses (1) the extent to which FirstNet is carrying out its responsibilities and establishing internal controls for developing the public safety network, (2) how much the public safety network is estimated to cost to construct and operate and how FirstNet plans to become a self-funding entity, and (3) what lessons can be learned from local and regional public safety network early builder projects.

[10] KPMG LLP, July 24, 2014. Independent Auditor's Report to the Secretary of Commerce and the FirstNet Board of Directors.

INDEX

D

E

F

G

H

I

J

L

M